Dynamics of
Library and Information Science

Dynamics of Library and Information Science

CHERIAN MATHEW

CYBER TECH PUBLICATIONS

4264/3, Ansari Road, Daryaganj, New Delhi-110002 (India)

Ph.: 011-23244078. Fax: 011-23280028

E-Mail: cyberpublicationsdelhi@yahoo.com

Dynamics of Library and Information Science

First Edition 2011

Published by G.S. Rawat
For Cyber Tech Publications
4264/3, Ansari Road, Daryaganj, New Delhi-110002
Ph.: 011-23244078. Fax: 011-23280028
E-Mail: cyberpublicationsdelhi@yahoo.com

Printed At Asian Offset Printers 9212182454

Contents

Preface

> "Little minds are tamed and subdued by misfortune, but great minds rise above them."
>
> —*Washington Irving*

Information and communication technology (ICT) has revolutionsed the world information system. Under its impact libraries of present day are quite different from the libraries of yore days.

As the title of this book suggests, this work is intended to furnish detailed information on dynamics of library and information science. The well-researched readings are collated in logical sequence. The following chapters make core of the study—Introduction; Information Science in Digital Age; The Use of Visual Media; Modern Librarianship and Information Science; Library Reference Sources and Computer Searches; Electronic Serials; Role of Intergovernmental Organisations; Issue of Other Electronic Library Materials; Deselection Issues in Digital Library; Appendices; Glossary and Bibliography etc.

Remarkably, the vital information is supported by fact and figures derived from research findings of leading library professionals from all across the world.

Definitely, this work will prove vade mecum to all library professionals besides academics, trainers and trainees in the field.

We are extremely grateful to all those men of letters whose works are cited or substantially made use of herein. The real credit this ought go to them all Our teachers, colleagues and friends have rendered yeoman's service by way of guidance, inspiration and assistance. We are deeply indebted to them also.

Finally we appreciate our publishers for evincing keen interest in this project and materialising it elegantly in the present shape.

We will welcome suggestions and comments for improving the contents of this which we will incorporate in subsequent edition with due acknowledgement.

—Author

1

Introduction

> "Within her automatic home
> The housewife lolls and lingers;
> No longer plagued by dishpan hand;
> Instead push button fingers."

We are living in a highly advanced (yet advancing) age of science and technology. Automation has come in a big way. Ours age is rightly called the 'knowledge age' or 'information era'. As such library science has become library and information science.

Before proceeding to the main theme, we should acquaint with 'information' and information science.

'Information' is such a widely used word, such a common-sensical word, that it may seem surprising that it has given 'information scientists' so much trouble over the years. The problem stems from seeking to discriminate among related words such as 'data', or 'knowledge' or even 'wisdom'!

Some writers in information science, however, have not been satisfied to treat 'information' as a noun but have tried to define it as a *process*—the process whereby facts and data are integrated into existing knowledge or transformed into organized bodies of knowledge. This seems to do violence to the language. The processes whereby data and facts are transformed into knowledge are the processes of perception, cognition and understanding. They are almost entirely mysterious to us, having resisted the most serious scientific investigation. Indeed, consciousness itself is not yet clearly understood.

To use the term 'information' to signify some cloudy set of terms in an attempt to give more solidity to the nature of information science hardly seems helpful. Other writers have carefully defined what *they* mean by 'information' in carrying out their research. The most popular definitions of this kind relate information to decision-making in a form such as, 'Information is that which removes uncertainty'.

Clearly, this is a *formal* definition because we all know that in the real world outside the experiment or the simulation we frequently receive communications of facts, data, news, or whatever which leave us more confused than ever. Under the formal definition these communications contain *no* information—party political broadcasts, perhaps.

The average person probably has little awareness of the terms information science and information research. They are related to the activities of a particular professional group (or, given the propensity to schism, particular groups); literature on the subject is found in specialized journals and rarely in the popular press; and it is written, at times, in a professional jargon that deters readers. Things may become clearly, however, if the word 'librarianship' is used. The word is appropriate because information science has developed out of librarianship and many of its research concerns are held in common with library research.

The Institute of Information Scientists in the UK has approximately 2,000 members and half of these are also members of the Library Association. In 1985 a conference of all professional bodies in the fields of information science, librarianship, archives management, and records management was held: an event which indicates the essential unity of the issues and problems faced by the different groups.

The branch of librarianship out of which information science has developed is generally known as 'special librarianship'. This term covers the activities of those working in specialized libraries and information units in business, industry, scientific research, government and local government. Its origins lie in the growth of industrial research activity during and following the World War I. Aslib, originally the Association of Special Libraries and Information Bureaux, was founded in 1924 and an American organization concerned with similar areas of work, the American Documentation Institute (now the American Society for Information Science) was founded in 1937.

It is pertinent to note that special librarianship and 'documentation' received a boost during and after the Second World War, partly as a result of the regeneration of industry, partly out a need to deal with vast quantities of industrial research and development documentation found in Germany, and partly as a result of the development of a new industry based on nuclear energy. That development resulted in such an increase in published reports and papers that a major new journal of summaries, *Nuclear Science Abstracts*, was established by the US Atomic Energy (USAEA) to disseminate information about information.

Remarkably, Fresh impetus to the generation of scientific and technical information was given by the launch of the first Russian Sputnik in 1957. The effect in the USA in particular was galvanic, leading to an upsurge in research activity and publication.

In fact, in both the nuclear energy field and in space technology research one feature caused problems for librarians in government and industry. This was the emergence of a relatively new form of publication, the research report. This form was not unknown in industry where internal research reports had always been produced by those firms with research and development departments. The new feature was the wider publication of such material. Sometimes the 'publication' was limited; for example, the United Kingdom Atomic Energy Authority restricted some reports to contractors in the industry. Both UKAEA and the USAEA, however, maintained depository collections in major public libraries.

The main problem in handling the vastly increased output of scientific and technical information was how to identify the subject content for effective retrieval of the material from storage. What in libraries had been known as 'cataloguing and classification' became known as 'information storage and retrieval' and a new field of information research arrived. In continues to thrive. During the Johnson administration in the USA (1963-1969), there was a great upsurge of social research associated with many aspects of social welfare and other issues. Much of this took the form of evaluation research on social programmes in the cities and, while not equal in scale to the volume of scientific information, the consequent growth of the literature was considerable and the semi-published report made its appearance in the social sciences.

Both developments and related events in the United Kingdom and in the agencies of the United Nations resulted in an interest in research into similar problems of information use and information storage and retrieval as in science and technology. Today, however, the systems that are created and used to control and disseminate information in industry, in government and in education make use of yet another force for change—the computer. This is not the place for a complete account of the role of the computer in information science. The aim here is simply to draw attention to its impact and to that of 'information technology'—a term which embraces computers, telecommunication systems, new means of storing information such as compact discs, and of communicating information such as teletext and view data systems.

Since the World War II, therefore, there has been a series of continuing pressures on libraries and information systems as a result of the developments noted above. The field of information science has evolved as a consequence of these pressures and research in the field aims to help in adapting systems to the pressures.

Information Science and its Changing Scope

What constitutes 'information science' is as much of a problem as the nature of information—naturally, since one depends upon the other. The definition used here is based on that given above:

> Information science is the study of the generation, organization, transfer, and utilization of information. It is concerned with the nature of information in general, with the channels or 'carriers' of information, and with the information user. It is concerned with all aspects of the design and evaluation of information systems and services, from public libraries to computer-based information retrieval systems.

As noted earlier, information science emerged originally out of the pressures placed on libraries and information services by the explosion of scientific and technical information. That bias exists to this day. Although research in information retrieval may now be concerned with such things as how children ask questions in libraries (Wanting, 1984) or how to devise a computer-based online catalogue for fiction (Pejtersen, 1984) there is a tendency for the literature to be very much concerned with scientific and technical information problems. This is partly a consequence of the dominance of scientific research over social science research in the scale of funding and in consequent publication. Some problems in scientific information have also been of continual interest, particularly those having to do with chemistry where chemical formulae and chemical structures lend themselves to highly structured methods of retrieval. The emergence of social science from its original neglect in favour of scientific information can be dated in the USA to 1950 and the University of Chicago (1950) report on bibliographical services in the social sciences. This beginning, however, was not followed immediately by research into problems of access to information, or different patterns of information-seeking behaviour. Interest in bibliographical aspects, that is, in the compilation of bibliographies and other guides to the social science literature, continued, however.

In the UK the beginnings can be dated to the start of the INFROSS (Information Requirements of Social Scientists) project in 1967. In the course of the INFROSS project Maurice Line and his colleagues surveyed the information-seeking behaviour of (chiefly) academic social scientists, and carried out a number of subsidiary studies.

INFROSS was followed in 1971 by DISISS (Design of

Information Systems for the Social Sciences) which was concerned chiefly with the growth of social science literature in a variety of fields, with the coverage of this literature by the abstracting and indexing services, and with implications for the planning of services (Bath University, 1980; Line 1981). During the INFROSS/DISISS period there were two major developments in bibliographic services to social scientists: the ERIC service (Marron, 1968) which covered information resources for education and drew upon the large volume of research commissioned by the US Government, and the extension of the Institute for Scientific Information's citation indexing into the social sciences (Garfield, 1972). In its early years the ERIC service attracted a good deal of comment, particularly on the quality of its indexing, and the entire service was subject to an intensive evaluation.

The *Social Sciences Citation Index* built upon the strength of its predecessor in science, and both services were quick to take advantage of that other development of the period, the computer. The terminology of the social sciences has always presented problems in information retrieval: not only does it use ordinary words in technical fashion (for example, 'class') but some of its technical terms, like 'bureaucracy', have changed their meaning subtly in common usage. As a result, a search may result in a set of documents which includes a large number of items which deal with, say, bureaucracy, but not in the sense anticipated by the user.

An additional difficulty is that adherents of different philosophical or ideological schools use the same term in different ways or with different associations. These issues were raised in connection with the ERIC service (Eller and Panek, 1968), were reviewed by Foskett (1963) and were the subject of research in relation to the sociology of education (Swift, Winn and Bramer, 1979).

Since 1967, therefore, there has been a growing awareness that the social sciences have information problems which are related to those in science and technology, in that they are the result of a similar 'information explosion'. The problems differ, however, because social scientific research differs from that in pure science. For example, controlled experiment is difficult, if not impossible, in social research. Directions of research may be more directly influenced by political considerations (witness Sir Keith Joseph's attempt dispose of the Social Science Research Council). And society and its constituents are continually changing in character, whereas, generally, the phenomena studied by science are more stable in their structures- -a molecule of hydrogen a century from now is likely to look very much the same as today's, while the nature of, say, the education system of the country could well be quite different.

Following the studies of the academic researcher in the social sciences, attention in the UK has focused upon the information problems of what might be called 'applied social sciences'. This era began with the study of local authority planning departments and planners in 1974 (White) and was followed by a major five-year project in the field of social services—Project INISS: Information Needs and Information Services in Local Authority Social Services Departments (Wilson & Streatfield, 1977; Wilson, Streatfield & Mullings, 1979; Streatfield & Wilson, 1980), and, simultaneously, by studies in education (Hounsell, *et al.* 1979). Subsequently, work was carried out in other local government departments (Grayson, 1978; Wilson, 1980a; Mullings, Francis & Wilson, 1980). In the USA over the same period the major project was probably URBANDOC (Sessions, 1971).

During the same period as the increase in interest in the social sciences took place there was a similar movement in relation to the citizen-at-large. In the 1930s there has been an interest in 'library surveys' culminating in an extensive review of the subject by McDiarmid (1940). At the end of the Second World War a major report on the public library user was carried out and reported on by Berelson (1949). In an attempt to provide a sound conceptual base for the study of the general information user the US Department of Health, Education and Welfare funded a study in Baltimore—Information Needs of Urban Residents (1973).

It is important to note that virtually none of the work carried out in the UK could have been done without the existence of the Office for Scientific and Technical Information and its successor the British Library Research and Development Department, which has the status of a research council for the field. Its resources have always been very restricted compared with other councils such as the SERC and the ESRC but there has been quite a high return on its investment in the shape of actual innovation, particularly in the adoption of computers for library tasks, as well as publication.

Whether one is concerned with the information behaviour of scientists or with that of social scientists it is clear that in either case social research methods will be employed. In the period immediately after the World War II, the model of social research employed by those researching the information behaviour of scientists was based on the then prevailing idea of quantitative research in social science, that is, the use of large-scale surveys intended to collect large amounts of data from which generalizations amounting to 'laws' similar to those in science could be derived.

This is understandable: those who carried out the work were likely to be scientists themselves and they saw their tasks as very much concerned with the description of identifiable aspects of behaviour. The work (such as that reported in the proceedings of the Royal Society Scientific Information Conference (Royal Society, 1948)) was also restricted almost entirely to a consideration of the sources and channels of communication used. There was little or nothing on the use made of information in scientific research or on the individual patterns of behaviour in information seeking.

The result of this methodological limitation was that progress towards some theoretical understanding of the concept of 'information need' was show. This fact was recognized by virtually every commentator on the subject from Menzel (1960) onwards. Generally, reviewers of the field have expressed disappointment in the results. The disappointment can be attributed in part to poorly chosen methods but also to:

1. a failure to realize how expensive survey research is, if done properly;
2. a consequent failure to do it properly because of insufficient funding;
3. lack of adequate insight into user behaviour before devising research instruments;
4. inappropriate choice of self-completed questionnaires as the data-collection method with resulting low response rates when the proper preparation and follow-up procedures (Robin, 1965) are not used;
5. lack of adequate theoretical frameworks to guide research;

6. lack of interviewer training and interview performance assessment resulting in data of unknown quality; and
7. use of library or information system perspectives on information use which may not be held by the people under investigation. (Wilson, 1980b)

As long ago as 1965 William Paisley commented on the lack of case studies in the field in his review of the literature (Paisley, 1965). In other words, the need for a more qualitative approach, that is one which would recognize the subjectivity of information use and the need to generate hypotheses about behaviour rather than simply test other people's ideas about behaviour, was recognized early. Little was done in response to this call however, and the early researchers in the field of information studies in the social sciences followed the path set out by the earlier researchers in science information studies.

Thus, although the INFROSS team carried out a small number of interviews, its approach was that of large-scale, quantitative data-collection using a lengthy self-completed questionnaire. In the 1970s, however, reflecting the increased awareness of the value of qualitative approaches in sociology, other researchers began to adopt more 'naturalistic', 'ethnographic', or phenomenological approaches. Reports on some of these constituted part of a special issue of *Social Science Information Studies* in 1981. Lawrence Stenhouse discussed the use of case studies in a project concerned with library use and access in academic sixth-forms noting that: 'Researchers have turned to case-study in the face of the difficulties which have been encountered in attempting to apply a scientific paradigm of research to problems in which human behaviour, action or intention play a large part.' (Stenhouse, 1981 : 221)

Harris (1981:251), in the same symposium, reported on an 'illuminative evaluation' strategy (Harris, 1981). This was employed in an action research project designed to produce teaching materials for the education of information users. Harris drew upon the work of Parlett and Hamilton (1976) and commented that: '[Illuminative evaluation] provided a convincing argument against the classic social science research model . . . It underlined the need to examine a wider range of contextual and environmental determinates of the success or otherwise of an education innovation.'

Earlier, in the same journal, Wilson and Streatfield had written on the use of structured observation in Project INISS and had noted that:

> . . . all methods of investigation are ultimately based upon observation. Either the individual observes his own behaviour and his own perceptual states and reports upon them within more or less artificially constrained frameworks (interview schedules, questionnaires, diary record sheets) or records of his information-seeking behaviour are kept (e.g. book issue records) from which deductions about the underlying needs are made. (Wilson and Streatfield, 1981: 174)

Wilson also contributed to the qualitative methods symposium and in his paper on Project INISS commented that: '...if anything is to be learned from the work, it is that a more sensitive approach to the collection of data and accounts will pay dividends in insights, theory, and practical ideas for improvements in information services'. (Wilson, 1981: 245)

Now we come to its relationship with other fields. The relationships between librarianship and information science has been discussed earlier and, in terms of the field of practice to which information science relates, this is probably the closest association. Nor would one wish to draw an artificial distinction between research and practice.

However, it is possible to look at the relationships between information science and other fields of research. We can begin by considering the definition quoted earlier and, hence, by dividing the discussion into three parts: the generation of information, the organization and handling of information, and the transfer and utilization of information.

In an essay such as this it would be inappropriate to deal with the literature in detail but in the paragraphs below one or two references are given for those with specific interests. In the case of the first of these there are strong links between information science issues and related issues in the sociology of knowledge, the sociology of science, and the sociology of various professional fields. One area of considerable interest is that which links 'bibliometrics' to research 'performance'.

Bibliometrics is the study of statistical regularities in various aspects of information generation and use. It has its origins in a study by Bradford (1948) which revealed the statistical distribution of periodicals borrowed from the Science Museum Library.

The so-called 'Bradford's Law of Scattering' was subsequently found to exist among citations to journals and with the advent of the *Science Citation Index* a great deal of work ensued on showing the universality of the 'law'. The idea has been misused (in this author's opinion) in seeking to show relationship between the quality of a journal or of a particular scientist and the extent to which that journal or scientist is cited by others. The second area, that of the organization and handling of information, is closely related to computer science. Although early work in information retrieval was closely associated with library classification and cataloguing, more recently it has become strongly identified with the use of computer systems.

Thus, most library 'housekeeping' functions, such as book ordering, cataloguing, book issue, and journal ordering and receipt systems, are now computer-based. In addition, the retrieval of information from large files of computer records is now a commonplace and an event such as the International Online Meeting in London can attract thousands of visitors to its exhibition to see the latest offerings from companies providing such services (Williams, 1979).

The actual retrieval mechanisms used in such systems are relatively crude, compared with the present state of knowledge and research in the field, but changes are taking place continually and as order computers are replaced and as novel computer architectures become more commercially viable the changes are likely to increase apace. Part of the information retrieval problem has close associations also with linguistics and computational linguistics. One continual problem has been the cost of 'indexing', that is, using human beings to select words and phrase to identify the subject content of documents. One solution has been so-called 'free-text searching', whereby the choice of words is made the responsibility of the searcher. The disadvantage here is that the words chosen by the searcher may not be a complete match for those used in the documents. One answer to this may be the development of more sophisticated computer systems based on the analysis of natural language.

Coming to the transfer and utilization of information, the links with other fields are diverse. For example, early work in the field of public opinion which led to the idea of 'opinion leaders' in the community has been replicated in the study of communication networks in scientific research laboratories, leading to the analogous idea of 'gatekeepers' (Allen and Cohen, 1969). Project INISS also paid specific attention to the communication activities in organizations and drew on that literature, and related to the study of information use to other aspects of the ordinary day-to-day work of people in organizations. In doing so the researchers acknowledged debts to such as Schutz (1946; 1970) and Berger and Luckmann (1966) for the relevance of the phenomenological viewpoint in studying the subjective aspects of the role of information in organizational life.

The subject of the utilization of information is clearly closely related to that of the diffusion of innovations and technology transfer and a number of studies have dealt with this area (Robertson, 1973; Rothwell, 1975; Shuchman, 1980). A special sub-set of problems relates to the economics of information. The emergence of this as a subject for research has had great deal to do with the economic recession. Libraries and information systems have been called upon more and more to justify their activities in economic terms and the idea of 'cost/benefit' equations applied to information services gained some currency in the 1970s (Martyn and Flowerdew, 1983).

The problem has proved virtually intractable, however. The chief problem lies in the nature of information: there is no standard measure of information according to which we can say that a person has become 'informed' to such-and-such a degree. What informs one, fails to inform another—what is news to one is old news to another. Researchers have also failed at times to distinguish between the 'exchange value' of information and its 'value-in-use'. We may be able to evolve methods for determining, but quantifying the value-in-use is likely to be a more difficult problem.

Summing Up

It is obvious from the above discussion that information science is a very diverse, and very active area of research. Whether it can be called a discipline is another matter, and whether it will have the resilience of the true disciplines of science is yet another matter. It may certainly be called a multi-disciplinary field and there is room for many different approaches to the problems with which it deals. Certain areas of research, however, may disappear into what might be called 'parent disciplines'. It seems that as workers in a particular area of research gain maturity and deeper understanding of their subject they draw more and more upon the theories and methods of the parents. When those in the parent discipline also become aware of interesting research issues in the field of information science, to which they can apply their own models, theories and methods, there is a tendency for the subject to be acknowledged as part of the parent discipline. The increased interest of those in computer science in the problems of information retrieval is a case in point. When information scientists first began to be involved in this area the number of computer scientists who were working in the field was very small.

Today the subject is a standard part of many computer science curricula. As yet, however, there has been not great tendency for the social sciences to take over parts of information science. The economics of information is regarded as a research topic in economics but many other areas discussed above appear to hold little interest for those in the parent disciplines.

There are exceptions to the rule, of course, but their solitary appearance in their fields proves rather than contradicts the rule. In fact most of the areas to which social scientific knowledge, theories, models and methods have been applied remain interesting research areas. Little is known about how information is used to help in the performance of research, or innovation in industry, or the performance of work in business, or many other areas.

How information from sources such as books, journals and library systems fits into the general information environment of an individual is still open to investigation. More remains to be done on the effectiveness of methods of disseminating information. The problem of effective storage and retrieval of information requires more work. The relationship of indexing and classification to linguistics have been explored but answers which are useful in practice await further understanding of human linguistic processes.

Here in the present book, we will discuss some salient features of modern library and information science.

2

Information Science in Digital Age

Library and information science is mainly concerned with the management of supplying information materials. As such libraries are repositories of knowledge.

How we can serve our clientele best? For this it is important to understand intellectual development and acculturation of our children. What is the role of information science in digital age?

We will address these issues in this chapter.

Much of a child's experience is formalized through schooling. Whether for reasons of economy or effectiveness, schools have settled upon learning out of context through media which are primarily symbolic. Schooling generally reflects the naive psychology which has been made explicit by Fritz Heider. The general assumption of such a naive psychology is that the effects of experience can be considered as knowledge, that knowledge is conscious, and that knowledge can be translated into words.

Symmetrically, words can be translated into knowledge; hence, one can learn, that is, one can acquire knowledge, from being told. Congruent with this is the belief that what differentiates child from adult is also knowledge and that the chief mission of school is to impart it by the formal mode of pedagogy. Concern for 'character' or 'virtue' centres not upon the school, but upon the home and the child's more intimate surroun-dings, the sources that provide models. The assumptions that knowledge was central to the educational enterprise and that it was independent of both the form of experience from which it derived and the goals for which it was used had several important and persisting effects on educational thought.

First, it led to a certain blindness to the effects of the *medium* of instruction as opposed to the content, a blindness that McLuhan has diagnosed well; and, secondly, it led to a deemphasis of and a restricted conception of the nature and development of *ability*. As the effects of experience were increasingly equated to the accumulation of knowledge, experience was considered less and less often the source of ability. Since knowledge was all, ability could be taken for granted—simply, one *had* abilities that could be used to acquire knowledge.

Abilities were, then, projected rather directly into the mind in the form of genetic traits. Culture and experience were both ignored as possible candidates to account for the development of abilities. The effect of this strange turn has been to downgrade the task of cultivating abilities in students, often thereby making schooling a poor instrument for the performance of this important task. Education critics have, of course, long attacked educational goals formulated in terms of the simple acquisition of knowledge.

Dewey's concern with the relationship between knowledge and experience has much in common with contemporary reanalysis. In his view, genuine experience involved the initiation of some activity and a recognition of the consequences that ensued. Experiences of this sort would result, Dewey argued, in the natural and integrated development of knowledge, skills, land thinking. Schooling, on the other hand, attempted to develop the three independently of each other and with little regard for the experience of which they were products.

No surprise, then, that schools frequently failed to achieve any of them. Dewey's revised conception of the relation between experience and knowledge reappears in the current attempts at educational reform which emphasize the role of process rather than content, or, more specifically, emphasize activity, participation, and experience rather than the acquisition of factual information. The contemporary critic and Dewey alike would attack the assumption that knowledge is acquired independently of the means of instruction and independently of the intended uses to which knowledge is to be put. That knowledge is dependent on or is limited by the purpose for which it was acquired has been illustrated in experiments by Duncker, by Maier, and by many other students of thinking and problem-solving. The conventional use of a pliers as a gripping instrument makes them difficult to perceive as a pendulum bob.

Knowledge *per se* does not make it possible to solve problems. The same appears to be true of verbally coded information. Maier, Thurber, and Janzen showed that information which was coded appropriately for purposes of recall was, as a consequence, coded inappropriately for purposes of solving a problem. Information picked up from experience is limited in important ways to the purpose for which it is acquired—unless special means are arranged to free it from its context. But this conclusion is at odds with the naive view that one can substitute 'instruction' for 'learning through experience.'

We must, then, re-examine the nature of direct experience and its relation to both knowledge and skills or abilities. Of course, the term 'direct' experience is somewhat misleading in that all knowledge is mediated through activity, and the resulting knowledge is not independent of the nature of those activities. But, if we consider both the knowledge of objects and events that results from experience and the structure of activities involved in experiencing, we may come closer to an adequate conception of 'direct experience'. We will then be in a better position to contrast it with mediated or, more accurately, the symbolically encoded and vicarious experience that is so important in acculturation.

Direct Experience

Psychology, mirroring an earlier physics, often begins an account of the nature of experience with the concept of the 'stimulus'. What occurs in behaviour is thought to be a reflection of the stimulus acting upon the organism. At a more abstract level of analysis, the shape of the effective stimulus is seen as the result of certain physical filterings or transformation of the input given by the nature of the nervous system and its transducers. This conception is much too passive and nonselective with respect to what affects organisms. Living systems have an integrity of their own; they have commerce with the environment on their own terms, selecting from the environment and building represen-tations of this environment as required for the survival and fulfilment of the individual and the species. It follows that our conception of physical reality is itself achieved by selective mediation. The search for a psychological account of behaviour must begin with the organism's activities and then determine the nature of the 'reality' sustained by that type of activity. It is a point that is explicit and central to Piaget's conception of adaptive behaviour in general and intelligence in particular: objects and events are not passively recorded or copied but, rather, acted upon and perceived in terms of action performed.

What does this view imply about the nature and consequence of experience? As we have said, we have a picture of reality that is biased by or coded in terms of our actions upon it; knowledge is always mediated or specified through some form of human activity. But note that any knowledge acquired through any such activity has two facets: information about the *world* and information about the *activity* used in gaining knowledge. In an aphorism: from sitting or chairs one learns both about 'chairs' and about 'sitting'. This distinction is reflected in ordinary language in the terms *knowledge* and *skill* or *ability*. There are, therefore, two types of invariants that are specified through experience.

The set of features that are more or less invariant across different activities may be considered as the structural or invariant features of objects and events that constitute our *knowledge* about those objects and events. Similarly, the set of operations or constituent acts that are invariant when performed across different objects and events may be considered as the structural basis of the activities themselves —that which we call *skills and abilities*. It is our hypothesis that 'knowledge' reflects the invariants in the natural and social environment while 'skills or abilities' reflect the structure of the medium or performatory domain in which various activities are carried out (see figure 1). Obviously, major significance must be attributed to *both* facets of experience.

Consider more specifically how both facets are realized in practice. The performance of any act may be considered a sequence of decision points, each involving a set of alternatives. These decision points are specified jointly by the intention motivating the act, the goal or end point, and the structure of the medium or environment in which the act occurs. A skilled performance requires that the actor have information available that permits him to choose between these alternatives. Problem-solving is a matter of trying out various means and assessing their contribution to the achievement of the end state. He must assess the means while keeping the end criteria in mind. It is a universal routine— in love, in war, in writing a paragraph or solving an equation, or, indeed, in managing to get hold of objects during the initial phases of the infant's mastery of reaching. From this point of view, mastery depends upon the acquisition of information required for choosing between alternative courses of action that could lead to a sought-after end. The most obvious way to acquire such information is through active attempts to achieve various goals in a variety of performatory domains. The most obvious way to learn about a country is to walk its streets, read its poets, eat its foods, work in its fields, and so on. In so doing, one will learn both about the country (*that* the country is poor or hilly, etc.) and how to proceed in the activities required to be of that country (*how to* mend a net or tell a story). This is surely what is meant by learning through one's own direct contingent experience.

Mediate Experience

But there are other ways to acquire information. From seeing a man struggle with his load, one can make some estimate of its weight. That is, one can experience vicariously or mediately. Psychological studies have repeatedly shown that learning can occur when neither of the primary conditions for learning through contingent experience—self-initiated action or direct knowledge of its results—is fulfilled. Bandura has summarized a wide range of data showing how behaviour can be modified and new behaviour patterns acquired by exposing the learner to modelling stimuli even in rather artificial laboratory situations. An illustrative experiment was performed long ago by Herbert and Harsh.

Two groups of cats learned to pull strings and open doors by observing other cats. One group of cats saw only the final errorless performances of cat models while the other group saw the early error-filled performances as well as the correct performances. Both groups of cats learned to solve the problems more quickly than the control cats, who learned only from their own contingent experience. But the cats that saw the error-filled performances learned more readily than those who saw only the error-free performances. Another alternative to learning directly is through symbolically coded information, that is, the information that is transmitted through the media—the spoken or printed word, film, diagram, and so on. It is learning through these symbolic systems that most readily substitutes for direct experience in formal schooling. Vygotsky and Bruner have emphasized the extent to which language provides the means par excellence for teaching and learning out of context, out of a situation in which action is in process and contingent consequences are most direct.

Language, as we shall see, provides an opportunity for acquiring knowledge which, while it is less useful for any particular line of action, has the advantage of ordering knowledge in a form compatible with the rules of abstract thought. We have, therefore, three modes of experience, which map roughly onto the three forms of representation discussed elsewhere as enactive, iconic, and symbolic: the first is related to direct action, the second to models, and the third to symbolic systems.

More important to our purposes is the fact that these three modes of experience map into evolutionary development. While all animals learn from contingent experience, primates are distinctive in their capacity for learning by observation—there is an enormous amount of observation of adult behaviour by the young, with incorporation of what has been learned into a pattern of play.

The human species is, of course, marked by its reliance on symbolically coded experience—so much so that the development of language is taken as the distinctive characteristic of the human species and the development of literacy in various symbolic codes is the primary concern of formalized schooling. It follows that these three forms of experience differ greatly in the assumptions they make about the organism; that is, they differ primarily in terms of the skills they assume and develop in the learner.

On the Acquisition of Knowledge

To this point, the burden of our argument has been to show that one can learn from three very different forms of experience and that these forms of experience, whether mediate or direct, qualify what is learned. The assertion to be examined here is that different forms of experiencing an object or an event can be mapped onto a common underlying structure—a coherent and generalized conception of reality. Information about a particular event, regardless of the activity or medium through which it is obtained, has in common the property that it permits the differentiation of that event from the alternatives with which it is in danger of being confused. Consider the experience of actually seeing a zebra with that of hearing the instructional statement 'A zebra is a striped, horse like animal.'

The same features detected in the act of discrimination

are specified in the statement; hence, they are informationally equivalent and they can both be mapped onto an underlying conception of zebras, horses, animals, and so on. This is not to deny that each mode has a residual uniqueness, but only to point out that they share a common structure as well. The range of topographically dissimilar forms of experience, including various forms of instruction, may be considered as various 'surface structures' which relate in their special ways to a common underlying structure of knowledge. Indeed, it is the very fact that information relevant to action can be acquired through means *other* than direct action itself that makes instruction possible.

Thus, one can learn to sail, perhaps only to a limited extent, through watching films and reading books. There is considerable evidence from controlled laboratory experiments to show that common learning results from different types of experience. A child can learn to construct a diagonal either through activity coupled with reinforcement, through an appropriate demonstration, or through verbal instruction. Others have shown that children can learn difficult-to-teach Piagetian conservation tasks through quite different training techniques. And it is well known that there is almost an infinite number of ways to teach reading. The problem is to specify as far as possible the structure of information in these various instructional forms of surface structures and to see how they each relate to the underlying structure described above. Once these forms or instruction have ben specified, it may be possible to indicate how each of them relates to the various technologies involved in their production and distribution.

All three forms of *instruction* can only be extensions of basic forms of interaction with the world and its symbols. They may be characterized as 'instructional' only when their use is marked by the intent of another person who for some reason, usually institutionally derived, accepts responsibility for the learner. *Learning from one's own contingent experience* can be regarded as instruction only in special circumstances, such as when the environment is intentionally prearranged by another person. The learner's role in this process is readily described as 'learning by doing', and the instructor's role is primarily that of selecting, simplifying, or otherwise ordering the environment so as to make the consequences of the action, the reinforcement, both obvious and safe.

The second form of instruction may be designated *observational learning*. The learner's role may be described as 'learning by matching,' and the instructor's role is primarily that of providing a demonstration or model and perhaps some feedback. The third form of instruction involves the *use of various symbolic systems,* including a natural language. The learner's role is primarily that of 'learning by being told' and the instructor's role is that of telling—providing facts descriptions, and explanations.

The three categories of instruction depend (as do the modes of learning on which they are based) upon the three modes of representing experience, namely, enactive, iconic, and symbolic. In our view, these forms of instruction and the related modes of representation reflect different surface structures of experience that share an underlying informational or *knowledge* structure.

Reinforcement

Firstly, consider the instructional effects of contingent experience, that is of reinforcement. Reinforcement broadly conceived is knowledge of the consequences of an act. Reinforcement assures a means of determining when an appropriate choice among alternatives has been made. Reinforcement, by its universality across species, provides a medium of information exchange whereby a Skinner can communicate with a pigeon, and vice versa, for organisms are potent sources of consequence for the actions of other organisms. This assumes that organisms respond systematically to the responses of others—though not necessarily by a simple calculus of good and bad outcomes. And, obviously, reinforcement mediates much interacting with the inanimate environment. But while the discovery of new knowledge may be dependent on our direct contingent experiences with nature and with other organisms, reinforcement has the limitation of being ambiguous in outcome. When a teacher reinforces a child for asking a question, the child may not know if it was the question-asking that she approved or the merits of the specific question. Reinforcement can rarely indicate the critical alternatives but can indicate the consequences of the final performance. Gutherie's cats, for example, did not know what aspect of their action in the puzzle box was critical for obtaining their release; hence they preserved many irrelevant ones. And given the fact that other human beings—with their obvious variability—are often the principal source of reinforcement, the ambiguity is confound. It is surprising how uncritical many people accept the idea of control of behaviour by reinforcement, in view of the constrained circumstances necessary for it to be effective at all.

And more important for instruction, a child obtains no relevant information from a reinforcement if he happens not to be considering the critical alternatives. Modern theories of discrimination learning move increasingly in the direction of distinguishing between feature selection (attention) and reinforcement to deal with this point. Given such considerations, one can account not only for the effects of this type of instruction but also for some of the anomalies in reinforcement theory. Three devices are widely used to render reinforcement less ambiguous. One is by immediacy: tagging the reinforce-ment directly to the act. The second is by disambiguating the feature of the stimulus to be attended to by placing it in a context that differentiates it from an alternative. The third is through 'scientific method,' by unambiguously assigning certain sequel to certain prior events so that the necessity of the conceptual link cannot be overlooked. This is typically the way of 'guided discovery' which, as with the other two techniques, relies on control of attention. In time, one who must learn by direct encounter comes to control his own attention in one of the three ways suggested: by keeping an eye 'peeled' for immediate results, by being selective in his scanning of features, and by attending to necessity and regularity of relationship.

Obviously, there is a technology and a form of materials that must go with the learning of such 'discovery or reinforcement skills.' It would be foolish to assume that such learning is not crucially dependent on education. If such were not the case, there would be far more learning from direct experience than there seems to be.

Modeling

One of the more transparent instructional approaches is that of meddling or providing demonstrations, an approach that makes up an important part of Montessori programmes. How is information conveyed through modeling? Complex acts cannot be imitated unless the performer already knows how to carry out the act. That is, modeling may initiate or instigate known behaviour but not, in any simple manner, produce learning. Yet, learning does occur in some situations. How can informations be conveyed appropriately through modeling? In line with the general theory advanced above, information permits a choice between alternatives. That is, consciousness of the alternatives is a necessary prerequisite for the pick-up or acquisition of new information. In another context it was reported that a Montessori teacher successfully modelled, for a three-year-old child, the process of reconstructing a diagonal pattern, a task that is normally solved only by four-or five-year-olds The demonstration consisted of showing the child each of the choice points, that is, the critical alternatives, and then indicating how to choose between them. The demonstration of *where not to go* or *what not to do* is important to the extent that those alternatives are likely to mislead the child. In this light, it is possible to understand the finding of Herbert and Harsh, mentioned earlier, that the cats who saw the error-filled performance learned more than those who saw the error-free performance. The latter performance deleted what the critical choice points or critical alternatives were. A final skilled performance does not render observable the critical alternatives; hence, the observer does not detect the information required to choose between them.

Good instruction through modelling depends upon the sensitivity of the instructor to the alternatives likely to be entertained by the child. Modelling or providing demonstrations is, therefore a skill to which most pedagogic theories are blind.

I.A. Richards provides an illustration of the pedagogic implications of such a theory: A teacher should know how to demonstrate the meanings of sentences and other things in ways which are at once unambiguous, memorable, and easily imitated... For instance, with a ball and a table, a skilled teacher can in two minutes make the primal opposition of *on-off* evident... A careless teacher in the same minutes can generate potential confusions with other distinctions to be handled with *to* and *from* and *up* and *over,* confusions which may later on make the learner's tasks far harder than they need be.

Just as providing clear demonstrations involves skill, it seems possible *that learning from demonstrations itself demands a skill;* depending upon its generality and utility, it may be a skill worth including in our educational aims (aside from the knowledge conveyed by that means). Elsewhere it has been argued that learning through modelling depends precisely on the capacity not so much to imitate directly as to construct behaviour from already mastered constituent acts in order to match selected features of the model—a procedure more like paraphrasing than imitating.

Verbal Instruction

Finally, consider language as an instructional medium. It is an instructional device *par excellence,* by virtue of the fact that a word indicates not only a perceived referent but also an excluded set of alternatives. Words function contrastively—they differentiate alternatives. The ordinary claim that 'words name things' overlooks the fact that words indicate or point to objects or events *in the implied context of the excluded alternatives.* This point may be grasped by noting that the name or the description of an event is determined by the contrasting alternatives. Thus, a large white block in the context of a small white block is called 'the large one,' while the same block in the context of a large black block is called 'the white one.' Reciprocally, hearing such a sentence, or any other instructional sentence, the listener knows about both the intended referent *and the likely alternatives.* That is, language is structured precisely in the way that is required for instructional purposes in general. For this reason, the instruction of literate subjects almost always involves language; when experimentally tested, such instruction competes favourably with that making use of reinforcement and ordinary demonstrations; language coding is less ambiguous, that is, it conveys more information than those other media of instruction.

But there are many ways in which language can specify an intended referent, and these ways provide a microcosm for examining the major premises of the instructional model presented in this paper. The point is that certain very different sentences covey the same information and hence are generally called paraphrases of each other, or synonymous sentences. Consider these simple examples:

The teaching of rules and strategies falls into a similar position; they are difficult to comprehend but they have wide generality. There is always a trade-off between these two factors, a trade-off that is reflected in an instructional rule of thumb formulated by Carl Bereiter (personal communication) to the effect that if the rules are easily stated and have few exceptions, teach the rule and let the learners practice applying it to various problems if the rules are not easily stated or have many exceptions, simply give practice on the problems and let the learners extract what rules they can for themselves.

The major limitation of language as an instructional medium, along with all cultural media such as graphs, diagrams, numbers, mime, and so on, is that the information is conveyed through a symbolic system that places high demands upon literacy in that medium. Further, the meaning extracted from those symbolic systems will be limited to the meaning acquired by the use of that symbol in the referential or experiential world. Stated generally, this limitation of language implies an ancient point that no new information can be conveyed through language. If the information intended by the speaker falls outside the listener's competence' the listener will interpret that sentence in terms of the knowledge he already possesses. It follows that instruction through language is limited to rearranging, ordering, and differentiating knowledge or information that the listener already has available from other sources, such as modelling, or through his own direct experiences. Parker has illustrated this point by showing the impossibility of verbally explaining perspective to the blind.

On the Acquisition of Skills and Abilities

Having said that knowledge from different forms of experience can map onto a common deep structure, we must now make plain that there are also differences. The most important non-equivalence among experiences of events in the three forms is manifest not so much in the knowledge acquired, but in the skills involved in extracting or utilizing that knowledge. It is true that common knowledge of zebras may be obtained from actual experience and from appropriate sentences, but the skills involved in the two cases are entirely different; it is obviously a skill to extract symbolically coded knowledge from a sentence, but it is no less a skill to discriminate zebras from horses, albeit a skill so overlearned that we fail to recognize it as such until we are faced with a subtler but equally 'obvious' discrimination such as that between Grant's gazelle and an impale. However combinable the outcomes, the skill of obtaining information by perceptual discrimination is a radically different skill from that of extracting the same information from language. The crucial issue for instruction, then, becomes one of deciding which skill one wishes to cultivate.

What of these skills ? As we pointed out earlier, they are frequently rendered invisible by our habitual focus on the knowledge specified through the activity. As we examine a rock by turning it over in our hand we are aware of the fact that we acquire knowledge about the rock, but the skilled manipulation that gave rise to the knowledge of the rock is transparent to us. Our earlier example suggested that in carrying out any activity, such as kicking a ball, we are learning not only about the ball, but about the act of kicking. Carrying out that act across widely divergent objects or events would be responsible for the development of a skill of wide applicability. But if we look at the general skills that make up our cognitive or intellectual ability, we see that they are marked by the same property.

Verbal, numerical, and spatial abilities reflect skills in such cultural activities as speaking and writing counting, and manipulating Euclidean space. Consider these skills in more detail. It is enormously to Piaget's credit to have insisted and demonstrated that the structure of any ability must be conceptualized in some major part in terms of 'internalized activity'. Activities one carries out in the physical world—rotating an object in space, lining up objects to form a straight line, ordering objects serially— come to be internalized or carried out mentally.

There is not only an internalization of operations, but an increasingly economical representation of diverse events operated upon. A face looked at from various angles comes to be represented as a single face. Even more important are the temporal ordering operations, which permit an appreciation first of physical order and then of logical relations. Once we can convert back from a changed state to our original one, we come to appreciate that such reversibility is a logical possibility or property of events and not simply an act one performs.

In turn, such operations make it possible to transform a novel event into a standard or base event or to convert some base event into a new structure more appropriate to novel contexts. The operations specified by Piaget were largely those appropriate to the manipulation of real objects in the physical environment. His basic premise is that their internalization not only produces the groundwork for logic, but assures that logic will be appropriate to the state of the world one experiences.

Such operations, consequently, have a wide range of applicability and appear to be almost universally relevant to problem-solving. But internalized activity related to the physical environment does not begin to describe the range of activities of the human mind. Specifically, it leaves out of account how we learn to cope with the cultural or symbolic environment. 'Learning from the culture,' like learning from physical activities, involves the act of picking up information to decide among alternatives; it also involves skills, and it also results, finally, in a biased knowledge of reality. Sentences, for example, to the extent that they are about something, carry information common to the other forms of experiencing and are comprehended and spoken in terms of those general underlying structures of knowledge we discussed earlier.

But the skills involved in using sentences are unique to the particular mode of expression and communication. The skilful use of a symbolic system involves the mastery of both its structure and its rules for transformation. Once mastered, these skills may be considered to be 'intelligence,' primarily because the range of their applicability is virtually open. This wide and expanding range of applicability is further indicated in the arts, which may be viewed in part as creative attempts to expand the limitations of a particular medium or symbolic system. These expanded symbolic systems may then be applied to nature, if appropriate, much as the binomial distribution was found to be an appropriate description of the range of human variability. In this way, our use of symbolic systems, like our practical activities, results in a version of 'reality' appropriate to the activity.

There is no objective reality to 'copy' or to 'imitate', but only a selection from that reality, expressed in terms of the kinds of practical and symbolic activities in which we engage. Thus, Nelson Goodman is led to say that 'the world is as many ways as there are correct descriptions of it.' Similarly, Cezanne pointed out that the artist does not copy the word in his medium but, rather, re-creates it in terms of the structure of that medium. So too with the ordinary man operating in the various symbolic systems of his culture.

Whorf was among the first to argue that we 'dissect nature along lines laid down by our native language.' But the process probably goes even beyond that, to something comparable to Gide's advising young poets to follow the rhymes and not their thoughts. For the child, as for the creative artist, the uses of the culture involve processes of expanding and refining the code, of defining 'lawful' or 'comprehensible' or 'possible' options as he defining 'lawful' or 'comprehensible' or 'possible' options as he goes. This is the heart of skill in the use of symbolic codes. Even our failures in understanding new media, as McLuhan has pointed out, come from a failure to recognize that they require different skills than does the medium they replace—as in going from an oral to a written code, or in going from print to television.

Man in culture, like the artist, is in continual search for ways of applying symbolic systems to his ordinary experience. Translation into a symbolic code such as logic or mathematics is even taken as the criterion for 'understanding' a phenomenon; to express the relation between temperatures, pressure, and volume in the form of an equation is to explain that relation. Hansen goes so far as to say that scientific knowledge consists of statements known to be true.

Yet a scientific and technological culture like our own has put a premium on translation into a few symbolic systems—written language as in literature and explanations, in logical and mathematical statements, and in spatial systems such as maps, models, graphs, and geometry.

We would argue that it is not only scholars, poets, and scientists who seek constantly to cast experience into symbolic codes. Our conjecture is that there is a form of metaprocessing that involves the constant reorganization of what we know so that it may be translated into symbolic systems. It is a matter of 'going over one's past experiences to see what they yield' both for the purpose of facilitating the communication that is required for the survival of the culture and for the purposes of rendering one's own personal experience comprehensible. We may label this form of activity as 'deuteropraxis,' or second-order information processing. Deuteropraxis is elicited not only by failed communication but also by a conflict and difficulties in attempting to carry out an action or solve a problem. It occurs whenever there is information-processing capacity available not demanded by the task in hand.

Deuteropraxis is involved in all translations of specific experience into general accounts. It can occur in any mode but it is clearly represented both by the poet's or essayist's search for the appropriate phrase or the summarizing aphorism and by the scientist's search for the most general mathematical statement. Merleau-Ponty has this in mind when he suggests that all intention wants to complete itself in saying. It is deuteropraxis that is responsible for the radical economization of the experience of the tribe or nation in a few great myths and, more generally, for the world view implicit in one's native language. It should not, however, be assumed that this process is simply one of translation. It more generally requires that the creator have more information available than was required for the ordinary experience of the event.

This can easily be seen in the difficulties one encounters in an attempt to draw a map of a well-known territory or to give a description of a friend's appearance. New requirements, new purposes, or new activities alter our perceptions of events; this is no less true when these activities involve those that have shaped or evolved by the culture, as in the arts, than when they involve various practical or physical acts. It follows that such symbolic activities as drawing an object, describing an object, or photographing an object require somewhat different information about that object than does the manipulation of the object. To the extent that these new forms of cultural or symbolic activity require previously undetected information about the world, the media of expression and communication are *exploratory devices*—a point of immense importance to an understanding of the child's acquisition of knowledge. Finally, deuteropraxis makes possible the organization of information into a form that is particularly appropriate for cultural transmission to the young. Since it is often difficult for the child (or an adult for that matter) to link an action with the consequences that follow, he is greatly aided by the deuteropraxis account of the event. Such accounts, whether in the form of an abstract equation, a principle, a noiseless exemplar, or an appropriate model, have the effect of 'time-binding' or virtually simultanizing temporal events and thereby surpassing ordinary experience.

The very accounts that render experience comprehensible render it inscrutable. But there are limits in the degree to which such representations, whether in language or other symbolic systems, can substitute for or extend ordinary experience. As summary of experience they are indeed powerful; as an alternative to experience they are sometimes woefully inadequate. One can learn or memorize the summary without having grasp of the information summarized. In *Portrait of the Artist as a Young Man,* Joyce tells how his teachers taught the young the aphorism 'Zeal without prudence is like a ship adrift' to show how instruction often falls wide of the mark. To some adult no doubt such a statement has meaning; it summarizes his own experience in a simple code. To the young it summarizes nothing. In large measure, the same is true of the great myths; to the extent that they summarize no experience, they convey little or no information. On the other hand, it is also true that aphorisms, like new vocabulary items, may serve as pointers from which experience is progressively assimilated. At an appropriate level, such instruction may be successful in aiding the assimilation of experience. Experience in this case instantiates the categories created through the symbolic code.

Frye makes a parallel point in regard to literature: 'criticism.... is designed to reconstruct the kind of experience we could and should have had, and thereby *to bring us into line with that experience* (p. 27).

Technological Realizations

Learning through contingent experience may be facilitated through rearranging the environment to render the consequences of activity more obvious. Laboratory experiments are prototypic attempts to simplify direct experience. Structured environments, simulations, toys, and authomatizing devices of various sorts have the advantages of both extending the range of a child's experience and making the relations between events observable or otherwise comprehensible.

Observational learning is realized through the provision of a model—'This is how you break out a spinnaker.' As we pointed out earlier, carrying out a performance for its own sake and carrying it out so as to instruct another are not identical. A good demonstration makes explicit the decisions made in the course of the activity—thus a good demonstration shows the student what not to do as well as what to do; a skilled performance makes these same decisions invisible. Technological media can greatly facilitate these processes by highlighting in various ways the critical points in the performance; slow motion or stopped action as well as descriptions and drawings (including caricatures) may have this effect. Such instruction, while it may convey some of the same information that would be apprehended through direct contingent experience (by virtue of its shared deep structure), is never complete in itself but, rather, specifies some of the major features to be looked for when actual performances are attempted.

That is, these forms of instruction rely heavily on prior or subsequent experience to instantiate the information. The instructional effects of a model are greatly increased by tying that demonstration to an appropriate symbolic representation as in the provision of a few mnemonic rules. The words 'keep your weight on the downhill ski' coupled with a demonstration will render the demonstration more comprehensible—the observer knows what to look for. But even this will not perfect the novice's performance; direct contingent experience is required to 'instantiate' the instruction. Indeed, it is probably not until such instantiation occurs that the proposition is fully comprehended. One says (after the first fall), 'So that's what he meant.' Hence, all modes of instructing are in some sense incomplete or inadequate for achieving full performatory power or efficiency, and knowledge in the last analysis is tied to one's own experience.

Learning through the various symbolic systems, including language, graphs, mathematics, and the various systems of visual representation, is realized through books, graphs, maps, models, and so on. These media make strong assumptions about the literacy of the learner. The properties of a 'good' explanation, description, or portrayal are complex subjects worthy of study in their own right. But to untangle the educational effects of these symbolic systems we again have to differentiate the knowledge of the world conveyed through the system from the skills involved in the mastery of the structure of the medium itself. Recall our aphorism: instructional means converge as to the knowledge conveyed but they diverge as to the skills they assume and develop. As to the knowledge conveyed, different systems are useful for the partitioning of alternatives or the conveying of information in a way that is fundamentally compatible with the information picked up from other types of experiences. You may learn that the stove is hot by touching it, by seeing someone recoil from touching it, and by being told that it is hot. Granted some level of literacy and granted that the learner has had some experience to instantiate the experience, the three forms are essentially equivalent. However, as to the skills they develop, each form of experience, including the various symbolic systems tied to the media, produces a unique pattern of skills for dealing with or thinking about the world. It is the skills in these systems that we call intelligence. The choice of a means of instruction, then, must not depend solely upon the effectiveness of the means for conveying and developing knowledge; it must depend as well upon its effects on the mental skills that are developed in the course of acquiring that knowledge.

The acquisition of knowledge as the primary goal of education can be seriously questioned. The analysis we have developed points to the contingent relationship between the knowledge acquired and the intellectual skills developed. To neglect the skills is to forget that they are the primary tools for acquiring and using knowledge—tolls that are critical for the child's further self-education.

Supply

Gauging the size of the literature provides an illustration of these problems. Statistics published annually in the *Library Association Record* give total numbers of education volumes published as 634 (in 1976), 539 (1977), and 536 (1978), but these figures are based on Dewey classes and exclude monographs on the teaching of specific subjects and relevant literature in the parent disciplines. The volume of journal articles can be gleaned from the coverage of the *British Education Index*, which has included references to approximately 3,000 articles annually since the early 1970s and draws on nearly 200 journals, chiefly of UK origin (Hounsell, Payne and Willett, 1978). These figures however mask a considerably larger corpus of documents. First, alongside commercially published monographs and nationally indexed articles is a large body of material in such forms as pamphlets, booklets, manuals and reports produced by educational and training institutions and organizations. Such documents often go unrecorded in the *British National Bibliography* and reliable statistics of them are difficult to come by. Second, the literature of the USA and of

Commonwealth countries is extensively used in some quarters (particularly by educational researchers and teachers of education as a field of study, and much more strongly in some area—e.g. educational psychology, economics of education—than in others). The coverage of the American Current Index to Journals in Education gives some indication of scale here: references to 22,866 articles were included in the 1978 volume (bringing the cumulative total since January 1969 to 186,217), and a total of 775 journals were being covered by May 1979 (Brandhorst, personal communication). Third, in looking at aspects of supply in education, the *kind* of documents produced is at least as important a factor as their volume. There is a richly varied mass of material which appears to have few common elements.

Similarly, convenient labels such as 'journals' or 'periodical' must by viewed with circumspection, since the terms are widely used in education to include such diverse publications as highly specialized research journals, the magazines of professional associations and trade union newspapers. Indeed, a ranking of periodicals contributing references to the *British Education Index* between 1973 and 1975 (Hounsell, Payne and Willett, 1978) showed that none of the first five items in the list (which together contributed almost one-fifth of all references) could be considered a scientific or scholarly journal when the usual criteria (such as refereeing by peers) are applied.

While the literature of education is abundant, diverse and diffuse, the level of availability in general terms is quite high. Several cooperative schemes have been established by the Librarians of Institutes and Schools of Education (LISE) to improve services to users in the geographical areas of England and Wales for which they are responsible (Humby, 1975); these include union catalogues of books and periodicals, cooperation in the storage of obsolescent books and the acquisition of overseas material, and union lists of stock on particular countries. And there have been similar cooperative efforts by the Annual Conference of Librarians in Scottish Colleges of Education. Foskett and Humby (1969) noted that 72% of requests made through the LISE scheme were satisfied.

This regional network is complemented by other national sources, the largest of which is the Department of Education and Science Library. This Library, which is open for reference and research enquiries, has a stock of 183,000 volumes and subscribes to 800 journals. Many other national organizations (the National Foundation for Education Research, the National Union of Teachers and the National Institute of Adult Education are only three such examples) have their own library and information services, while there is a small number of more specialist libraries such as the Language Teaching Library of the Centre for Information on Language Teaching and the English Teaching Information Centre.

Not all kinds of material are widely available since some collections exclude specific categories of information, for example the DES collection does not include school textbooks, and documents such as curriculum materials, policy documents and progress reports on research are often difficult to trace. An interesting initiative has been the introduction of *CORE*, a new microfiche journal which publishes full-length versions of material such as conference proceedings and full-length versions of material such as conference proceedings and full-length research reports which may not be readily available elsewhere. Cooperation and a readiness to link stock to bibliographical sources have helped to establish good inter-library loan services. For example, the Inter-Library Loans Service at Boston

Spa has the entire collection of microfiche represented in the American *Resources in Education*, and has been willing to extend its holdings of journals to cover material appearing in the companion ERIC journal, the *Current Index to Journals in Education*, as comprehensively as possible. At the same time, a tradition of treating comparative education as one of the subjects studied in most teacher training courses has made a considerable contribution to the general availability of foreign-language material, further aided by the publication by LISE of union lists of stock on education in specific countries.

This favourable picture should be qualified in two ways. Firstly, ease of availability is closely related to status and institutional affiliation; those working in academic institutions are likely to perceive the inter-library loans service as rapid, efficient and extensive, but others (such as schoolteachers) to whom use of these institutions' libraries has been extended, may find their access to inter-library loan facilities tightly constrained. Similarly, users of public libraries will in many cases be at a considerable disadvantage compared to those in academic institutions.

Second, while the availability of foreign-language material is at least satisfactory, there has been no major effort to translate, summarize or synthesize this literature in any systematic way, and in those few instances which are the exception, the driving-force has tended to be the influence of a particular school of thought (e.g. French sociology of education) rather than an interest *per se* in the perspectives of other nations and cultures.

Demand

The potential market for educational information in the United Kingdom is large and varied. One detailed study (Hounsell, Payne and Willett, 1977) indicated that in excess of three-quarters of a million people are professionally employed in the education and training services. Breaking this figure down into the broad categories adopted by Mersel, Donohue and Morris (1966), by far the largest professional grouping is *teaching* (with over 700,000 staff employed) followed by *administration and ancillary services* (almost 50,000) and *research and scholarship* (4,000). Though often used, a tripartite categorization of this kind serves to conceal differences both within and across categories. An example of the first kind is the administrative category, which embraces professional sub-groups as diverse as local education authority advisers, central government administrators, teachers centre wardens and educational correspondents. And an important across-category difference is that of employer or employing institution: as far as demand for documents is concerned, the university teacher seems likely to have more in common with the university-based researcher than with the schoolteacher, the adult education lecturer, the teacher in the Prison Education Service or the industrial training officer.

Differences in the kinds of demands made by these various subgroups is in part a function of the diversity of the education and training services. While some questions (e.g. teaching method, models of course design) are manifestly of interest across a broad spectrum of groups, others tend to be viewed largely within the framework of specific parts of the system. On the one hand, differences in the age of ability levels of the students are inevitably one distinguishing factor in interest (clearly the educational concerns of the primary teacher are significantly different for those of the tutor of undergraduates); on the other, primary education, secondary education, higher education, adult education, further education and industrial training comprise more or less discrete organizational sub-systems each with its own characteristic rationals, procedures, etc. Subject affiliations are also a strong source of demand differences, since for many (if not most) teachers their subject or discipline is a more powerful reference-point than the kind of institution in which they are employed or the age of ability-level of the pupils or students for which they are responsible. But if these differences make for variations in the direction of demand, perhaps the greatest single area of difference is in *intensity* of demand. It is generally accepted that the highest level of demand is from researchers and that here, as in the United States (see for example Nelson, 1972), the journal article is the chief medium of communication between researchers. Since as we have seen, the number of educational journals in the English language alone is very high, monitoring through bibliographical sources is especially important for the researcher, and British sources include not only the *British Education Index* but three abstracting journals and over thirty current-awareness services (Hounsell, Payne and Willett, 1978), many of which have specialized interests and audiences which extend beyond the narrow confines of research.

Brittain (1970, p. 120) has suggested that education 'is perhaps better covered by bibliographical tools and information services than any other social science', but the value of this wealth of information sources to those other than researchers is questionable, if not largely irrelevant. Indeed it can be argued that while the myriad assortment of documents which make up the primary literature generally represent responses to a host of different users' needs, the secondary literature is directed almost overwhelmingly towards an academic audience.

And while the needs of teaching and administrative groups have been little researched and are often poorly understood. Of those two groups, administrators are by far the most neglected. There is limited evidence from a recent study (Hounsell, Payne and Willett, 1979) that topics of interest change rapidly and that administrators have little time to look for information or to read it. The needs of teachers have been better documented (see for example Cane and Schroeder, 1970; Information Requirements . . . 1971; Hounsell *et al.*, 1980) though the studies undertaken have tended to focus on research and development information rather than on subject-based curriculum and teaching materials.

The Lancaster enquiry (Hounsell *et al.*, 1980) yielded similar findings. Four out of five of the teachers surveyed felt that a gulf existed between themselves and researchers, chiefly because of the tediousness of research reports, research jargon and poor dissemination of findings to schools. And while almost all of the teachers thought that being well-informed about educational research and development was important, there was a division of opinion on whether teachers were well-informed. The main obstacles to keeping up-to-date were a lack of time, both to read and to look for information, and a lack of advice. However one-third of the teachers had made a specific enquiry for information in the recent past, and more than half of the teachers had been influenced by research which they had read or heard about. There was also evidence that communication was by no means predominantly informal; books and reports (together with teaching colleagues) emerged as the most popular sources of information, and main-steam periodicals (such as the Times Educational Supplement) were widely read.

Two other findings are of interest here. The first of

these is that information was more likely to be found useful it rooted in the experiences of individual teachers or specific schools. This provides an interesting contrast to the perspective of Allison (1974, p. 194), writing as a scholar-researcher, who criticizes the educational literature for the very reason that 'personal experience seems to be the touchstone of truth'. The second is that there was a significant relationship between length of teaching experience and use of information: the more experienced teachers were more likely to have been influenced by research, to have made specific enquiries for information, to look for information beyond the immediate confines of the school, and to make greater use of periodicals and libraries.

It should be clear from the arguments presented in this paper that, in so far as educational documents are concerned, the scope for global observations on the relationship between supply and demand is strictly limited, principally because of the existence of a great variety of professional sub-groups, each of which would seem to have its own characteristic patterns of demand and use. And it follows that even where a satisfactory match between demand and supply can be identified—as in the case of researchers—the temptation to adopt this as a model which might be applied to other, less well matched groups of users should be resisted. A successful model of communication for one group may be quite inappropriate for another. It is not simply a question of differences in the kinds of documents demanded, but of their orientation, the relative weight assigned to theoretical rigour and practical reference and—most importantly—of the strength of demand.

For it is difficult, certainly in the immediate future, to envisage a situation in which the pattern of commitments of administrators and teachers would change so significantly as to afford them anything approaching the researchers' opportunities to keep abreast of the literature. Nor, without a better understanding of the role of new information within their professional duties, do we even know whether becoming better 'informal' would have more than a negligible impact on their professional effectiveness.

It should also be recognized that any other measure of improve the supply-demand match may by itself make little headway. In our study of educational information and the teacher (Hounsell *et al.*, 1980) we concluded that a major improvement would come about only as a result of a strategic combination of measures which had regard to conceptions of the role of information within the teaching profession, user education in initial and in-service training, the establishment of a system or network of provision, the creation of appropriate information services, and dissemination strategies.

This is not to say that the situation is static, or that certain measures might not have some impact. Britain has been closely involved in the work of EUDISED (European Documentation and Information System for Education) (see for example Macgregor, 1975) which has resulted in a number of technical reports, a multilingual thesaurus, and registers of research in progress and experimental bulletins on periodical articles and audio-visual materials. There is also growing acknowledgment that research and development information seldom reaches practitioners who might learn most from it, and there have been recent initiatives by bodies such as the Schools Council, the National Foundation for Educational Research and the Social Science Research Council examine or to improve dissemination.

These efforts undoubtedly need to be linked to an intensive study of the use of information by practitioners, using a more qualitative methodology than hitherto which also takes account of the context in which those being studied work and communicate with one another. The main stumbling-block here is the problem which besets information development in general; how is one to assess the potential impact of information, assuming that information could be presented in a form that the practitioners found both accessible and digestible? A valuable start could be made, even on a small scale, by experimenting with highly selective information services, perhaps based on extended summaries.

3

The Use of Visual Media

Traditionally in teaching and learning process books and other printed materials were/are used. Libraries are equipped with useful reading materials in different firms. But with the emergence of new information technology, libraries are also going digital—as such now we have digital libraries or electronic libraries. These forms of library collections have paved the easy and more convenient way of teaching and learning.

Here in the present chapter we will give an account of the use of visual media. This narration is based on experiences of a teacher.

Many of us desire to employ the visual media in the teaching of psychology. The typical reasoning behind this desire, which is more frequently expressed than practised, is, however, not well throughout. Is it indeed the case that a picture is worth a thousand words ? Is a graph necessarily better comprehended than a verbal description ? Why is *Clockwork Orange* more revealing than, say, a scientific analysis of brutality ? Why bother to teach group processes through *Twelve Angry Men* rather than read the transcript?

It appears that we should attempt to answer such and similar questions in the same way we teach our students to do it. Namely, to begin with a *theory*. Specifically, we need a theory that sorts out the relevant elements, that differentiates between fact and fiction, and which is sufficiently general to guide future questions.

The rather common answer to the kinds of questions is frequently as follows: (a) A-V materials can reveal unique and helpful contents, and (b) they offer that content through concrete, vivid experiences which are (for some unclear reason) superior to texts, lectures or discussions. Similar potentialities are often attributed to the technology associated with certain media (e.g. the ease of transmission through CCTV) or to the didactics associated with them (e.g. immediate feedback or better structuring of the materials).

Such answers confuse quite a number of issues. For example, contents are by and large transferable: You do not have to watch *Equus* in a film, you can read it: you do not have to observe an interview with Karl Jung on video-tape as one can read its content to you aloud. Thus, we confuse some unique attributes of visual media with non-unique ones. Similarly, we implicitly assume that different media offer different experiences, and yet we see them as alternative means to the *same* ends, particularly the acquisition of factual knowledge (Olson, 1976).

Uniqueness in Media

First, then, let us raise the question of what is unique to each medium and what is the *essential* difference, i.e. neither trivial nor accidental correlate, between them?

We have reason to argue that the essential difference between media is neither their contents (which itself is an outcome of a more fundamental difference), nor the available didactics, but rather *their modes of gathering, packaging and presenting information, that is: their symbol systems*

(Goodman, 1968: Gardener *et al.,* 1974; Salomon, 1979a). To presently avoid unnecessary philosophical debate and in the service of brevity, let us speak of media's 'modes of presentation' and symbol system as equivalent. Indeed, remove cartography from maps, language from texts, pictoriality from film, movement from ballet, what are you left with? Not much.

Quite clearly media's symbol systems, or modes of presentation, owe much of their development to technological innovations. More detail and finer depth presentation became available through copper engravings, new 'statements' could be made once the zoom lens was developed, and a new 'language' becomes possible now with the development of holographs. Yet, let me remind you that it is not any technology *per se* that affects learning (e.g. Mielke, 1968; Schram, 1977).

Rather, the new symbol systems and the new combinations of old ones that become possible with new technological inventions, enable us to gather, package and present new aspects of knowledge. Thus, media's unique symbol systems and the unique combinations thereof are the very essence of media: they develop with the advent of new technologies and make new kinds of content available. If media's symbol systems would be only mediators between technology and presentable content, then we would not have to dwell on their psychological import at all. We would concentrate on what media's contents could do for us.

However, following Olson and Bruner (1974), Olson (1976) and my own work (Salomon, 1974, 1976, 1977, 1979b), I want to argue that *media's symbol systems have their own important effects on people's minds.* And it is these effects that, once understood, can lead us to develop novel ways of using the visual media to serve new educational functions.

Let us begin with the assumption that while the contents of messages address our structures of knowledge, the means of conveying the knowledge, the symbol systems, address our mental skills (Olson and Bruner, 1974). Thus, one can speak of intelligence as skill in a medium. When you read a book, see a play, watch a film or examine a painting, you may gain knowledge. However, the very *activity* of reading, film-viewing, map-reading or listening, *taps different kinds of mental skills.* As Olson (1978) writes: 'Skills are frequently rendered invisible by our habitual focus on the knowledge specified through the activity' (p. 6).

And as Gombrich (1974) shows, numerous skills, often 'automatic' ones (LaBerge and Samuels, 1974) are involved even in reading a regular black and white photograph. We do not read it as representing a gray, flat and framed world. Salomon and Cohen (1977) have shown that different coding elements within the filmic symbol systems, such as spatial editing, zooms, logical gaps and close-up-long shots, call upon different kinds of mental skills. Hence, film-viewing is a skilled activity, and the specific kinds of coding elements it uses tap differential abilities. Spatially able students extract more knowledge from elements that distort known conceptions of space, while students with better mastery of temporal abilities extract more knowledge when time is being distorted.

As Snow *et al*. (1965) have shown long ago, there are more general aptitudes which are called upon when all kinds of film are shown, and these aptitudes are less relevant when face-to-face instruction takes place. Meringoff (1978) has shown that aside from the above, televiewing leads small children to extract different kinds of knowledge than listening to the same story when read aloud. Listening also calls for the generation of more personal inferences than televiewing. Two implications seem to follow. First, as different coding elements within a symbol system call upon different skills, so do whole symbol systems, only on a larger scale. We would expect students with different clusters of aptitudes to benefit differentially from different symbol systems (provided our media presentations employ their unique symbolic potentialities).

This, of course, is much in line with the known conceptions of aptitude—treatment interactions (ATI), as formulated by Cronbach (1957); Salomon (1971) and Cronbach and Snow (1977). I will relate to this as a *first order interaction* between symbol systems and learners' aptitudes. The second implication is somewhat more complex. Traditionally, we attribute to some symbol systems characteristics of 'concreteness' and 'iconicity,' and to others 'abstractness' and 'arbitrariness,'. However, following the philosophical works of Goodman (1968, 1978) and my own analyses (Salomon, 1979a), it appears that symbol systems are 'iconic' or not relative to the way one represents the depicted or described entity *mentally*.

We use different kinds of symbol systems *mentally* to represent the world to ourselves and to manipulate it in thought (Paivio, 1971: Kosslyn and Pomerantz, 1977). External modes of representation can thus be closer or farther away from the internally used once. A verbal description of an activity or process which you, for many cultural, developmental, situational and personal reasons, represent to yourself as visual images, is remote from its cognitive counterpart. Similarly, if we should try to present the ideas of this article through, say, a pictorial symbol system, we would be using a rather remote (i.e. non-iconic) 'language', because many people prefer to think about such issues in terms of internal propositions.

It follows, then, that 'iconicity' is *not* an inherent attribute of a symbol system but a function of the 'distance' between it and one's internal mode of representation. And as such modes differ with content, maturation, preference, etc., also 'iconicity' or 'abstractness' are flexible, relative, quantities. Statistical formulae are neither 'abstract' nor 'arbitrary' for one who thinks in terms of statistical formulae. When the 'distance' between external and internal modes of representation is large one needs to activate processes of *recoding,* that is, invest mental effort in translating the external symbolic mode into the internal, preferred one.

When, then, the information is new, its quantity large, and the recoder not well skilled, much of the information gets lost. But, barring extreme cases, the more one needs to recode, not only does he/she learn more, but he/she also draws more heavily on his/her own mental schemata (e.g. Kane and Anderson, 1978; Gallagher, 1979). This brings us back to our second implication.

Television and film may often be easier for processing (not only for children) because one often represents certain entities through imagery. Pictorial symbol systems thus as much of the recoding effort required by, say, language. But if pictorial systems require (or rather, *allow)* less recoding, then they may lead to less learning. They also often allow us to draw less upon our own mental schemata, as Meringoff's (1978) study shows. Such would not be the results for learners who think of the same entities in terms of internal propositions. For them, pictorial systems may address a less preferred internal symbol system, require more recoding, and thus lead to more learning.

An interaction between external and internal modes of representation which results in more or in less skilled reocding, in more or in less learning, and in heavier or lighter reliance on one's own mental schemata. Unlike the first order one, the second order interaction is highly variable, depending on the content presented, the task to the performed, one's preferred cognitive systems, etc.

The Cultivation of Skills

Thus far we have dealt with the different kinds of mental skills that symbol systems call upon and the different amounts of mental recoding they seem to require. But media's symbol systems appear to have other, far more pervasive effects on learners. We will mention here two such effects: the cultivation of mental skills and the cultivation of new internal modes of representation.

If mental skills are involved in extracting knowledge from symbolically coded messages then such skills can and do develop as a result of media's requirements. From watching the film *The Phoenix* you not only acquire knowledge about the emergence of leadership, but also exercise certain film-related mental skills. The fact that we are often unaware that skills are needed only suggests that they are already well developed and can be used 'automatically'.

Yet, as Kintscha (1977) points out: 'Novels or movies are easier when the natural order of events is maintained than when they are full of flash-backs and reversals, but since the latter invite deeper processing, they are more interesting to read or watch' (p. 315).

They are indeed more interesting, and may render also more unique information because they call upon not yet 'automatic' skills.

In a series of experiments and field studies (Salomon, 1979b) we could show that when specific coding elements of film—such as close-up—long-shot, varying spatial positions or changing points-of-view—are used under common learning conditions, they lead to improved mastery of relevant skills. Quite clearly, when coding elements call upon certain skills, they can cultivate those best in learners with a modest initial mastery of the skills. Skill-cultivation by activation cannot benefit a learner with no, or very poor, initial mastery of the skills. When skills such as relating-parts-to-wholes, spatial imagery, changing-points-of-view and possibly others, show improvement through activation, they may also transfer as *mental tools* to new instances.

We do not know as yet which skills transfer more widely and which ones begin as, say, film-literacy and stay untransferable to other symbol systems. The well-known rules of transfer-of-learning seem to apply here, as elsewhere. Transferability would depend not only on the nature of the skill but also on the nature and availability of other instances to which the skill can be transferred, and on one's awareness that a skill—such as changing spatial perspectives—is applicable to totally new instances.

While we know that the filmic symbol system can be made to cultivate skills, we do not as yet know their potential transferability.

Let us turn now to the effects of symbol systems on the development of internal modes of representation. If we are willing to accept the assumption that people represent the world to themselves and manipulate it mentally through a number of internal symbol systems, we cannot avoid the possibility of interdependence between external-communicational and internal-cognitive symbol systems.

Numerous psychologists, aestheticism and philosophers (e.g. Bruner, 1964; Brown, 1965; Von Bertalanffy, 1965; Perkins and Leondar, 1977; Vygotsky, 1978; Eisner, 1978) have argued time and again that internal symbolism develops, in part at least, as a counterpart of external-communicational symbol systems.

There is little disagreement that language serves prominently in thought. Even without going as far as Whorf or even Vygotsky (1978), one could agree with Schlesinger (1977) that thinking emerges from interactions with a language community. Ultimately although not initially, one learns to 'compute' thoughts in those linguistic structures which serve in the production and comprehension of speech.

Briefly, the linguistic symbol system serves as a system of mental tolls which operates in internal manipulations of the world. And it does this apparently in two ways. It summarises, labels and internally represents already acquired knowledge, thus it serves a *representational function* (Olson, 1978).

For example, acquiring new concepts such as 'intrinsic' and 'extrinsic' motivation allows the student to go over, so to speak, his or her past experiences and subsume them under these concepts. The concepts come now to represent in the student's mind a vast array of past experiences, observations and bits of knowledge. But a symbol system such as the linguistic one serves also to guide and direct our exploratory and data-gathering behaviour, thus—to accomplish an exploratory function as *epistemological devices* (Olson, 1978).

Once the student in the above example has learned about the two sources of motivation he or she can now start noticing events and behaviours to which he/she attributes hidden causes he/she would not have attributed before. Furthermore, he/she begins to notice things which he/she did not notice before.

Let us embed these arguments into Neisser's (1976) spiral model of perception and cognition. According to this model, one's mental schemata—including different kinds of symbolic representations—direct our perceptual exploration. Exploration, in turn, samples, constructs and provides meaning to external stimuli which are then incorporated into the schemata and change them accordingly. Note that the acquisition of externally-provided concepts, labels, and other symbolic representations (e.g., a graph, a picture) changes one's relevant schemata.

In this sense they serve in what we called a representational capacity of knowledge already stored in the schemata. But, once acquired, such symbolic representations begin to guide perception, information-gathering and comprehension, thus to serve in a epistemological capacity. Language that figures in thought comes from the outside world of communication. How then is it transformed from a communicational symbol system into an internal, mediational one? Vygotsky (1962) and later Luria (1976), working within a Marxian inter-actionist framework, suggest that language is interiorized, or internalized, by the child. Luria writes: 'Children assimilate language—a ready-made product of socio-historical development—and use it to analyse, generalize and encode experience'. Not only words but also grammatical structures are interiorized: thus, 'humans have at their disposal a powerful objective tool that permits them not only to reflect individual objects or situations but to create objective logical codes'. Vygotsky does not claim that thought is *created* by language, as Whorf would have it. The internalization of language results in a *reorganization* of thinking into higher order functional systems.

Still, *internalization* serves as the key process. Even Fodder (1975, p. 83), the opponent of such views, find sit necessary to qualify his general argument by stating that though it might be admitted that the initial computations involved in first language learning cannot themselves be run in the language being learned, it could nevertheless still be claimed that a foothold in the language having once been gained, the child then proceeds by extrapolating his boot straps: the fragment of the language first internalized is ıtself somehow essentially employed to learn the part that's left.

This process eventually leads to the construction of a representational system more elaborate than the one the child started with and this richer system mediates the having of thoughts the child could not otherwise have entertained. But language is not the *only* symbol system that participates in thinking. Miller *et al.* (1970) have tried to replicate one of Luria's studies concerning the use of externally provided verbal instructions for self-regulation by three and four-year-olds. Although they failed to replicate Luria's findings, Flavell (1977) did not reject the internalization conception.

Rather, he interpreted the failure as resulting from the assumptions that only internalized *language* can serve for self regulation. Other, non-linguistic modes could serve equally well, or even better, for some children. Shepard (for example, 1978) has shown how important non-linguistic internal codes are in solving spatial problems. The work of

Furth (1966) with deaf children shows that, even in the absence of a well-mastered language, thinking can be relatively well developed, suggesting that language is only one of many ways whereby thought is carried out. Could other, non-linguistic symbol systems become part of our cognitive apparatus in a way that resembles that of language? Could a child learn to think in, say, *graphical codes* as he does with language?

Hatano *et al.* (1977) have shown that expert abacus users seem to have internalized the operations of the abacus. This is suggested by the observation that users at intermediate levels still need to use visible finger movements to accompany mental computations.

When prevented from using their fingers, such uses perform significantly less well. Experimental intervention of this kind has no appreciable effect on expert users. The finger movements of intermediate users of the abacus appear to be very much like egocentric speech, which, according to Vygotsky, is 'overt thought preceding inner speech'. Both are overt activities in the process of becoming totally internalized and covert.

Here, however, we face a possible pitfall. The analogy between the internalization of language and non-linguistic systems may be misleading inasmuch as language is acquired through active *interaction* while most non-linguistic systems are only *observed.* Only a few people interact through pictures, filmic-codes or cartography. Could the latter be acquired through observational learning? Observational learning of modeled behaviours is a learning procedure that 'enables people to acquire large, integrated patterns of behaviour without having to form them gradually by tedious trial and error' (Bandura, 1977, p. 12).

However, modelling is not limited to overt physical acts. Observational learning also occurs with linguistic skills, conservation of liquids, attitudes, and emotional responses (Bandura, 1977). Underlying *all* these, according to Bandura, are common processes of attention, internal coding, rehearsal, and reinforcement by self or others. The teaching potential of modelling need not be limited to observational learning of behaviours of humans nor to the informative contents of 'symbolic modelling'. Indeed, this is very much in line with Bandura's explanation of the role of observational learning in language acquisition. However, lest we oversimplify the case by arguing that all symbol systems encountered in the media can be internalized and used as coding elements in thought, we must at least show *why* they are learned. The internalizability of codes must surely depend on their function. Once we have a plausible (if speculative) explanation, we should be able to generate specific hypotheses pertaining to the conditions in which specific coding elements are internalized.

Again a verbal construction or spatial depiction, to be learned and used in perception and thought, needs to accomplish some useful function for the learner. It must promise a solution for a perceived difficulty. As Cole and Scribner (1974) theorize with respect to cognition and cultural differences, a skill is evoked and potentially cultivated within the context of functional demands. Thus, for a coding element to become a tool of thought, it must accomplish some useful cognitive function. It needs to accomplish for the learner something that the learner cannot perform on his own yet needs to perform.

Indeed, this is precisely what we have found in our experiments (Salomon, 1974, 1979b). When subjects are shown a filmic operation which *overtly models* an operation—

such as rotations in space, changing points of view, zooming, or laying-out objects—the ones with poorer mastery of such operations seem to imitate and internalize the operations. Thus, the overt model seems to *supplant* a mental activity which can then be internalized, provided it has not been well-mastered beforehand. The modelled operation seems to accomplish for the students an operation they cannot yet perform themselves and which does not easily translate into another, say, linguistic code. Our students have learned to use these new symbolic operations in their cognitive representational system and to transfer them to new instances. They have learned to think in terms of filmic codes.

As we have found similar evidence also in field and cross-cultural studies *outside* the laboratory (Salomon, 1976; Salomon, 1979a), we feel quite confident in arguing that the symbol system of a medium such as film can serve as a cultivator of mental abilities and internal modes of representation. Quite clearly, though, media's symbol systems can cultivate mental skill only if (1) they are sufficiently unique, i.e. do not easily map upon alternative systems (as does the Morse Code with respect to language), and (2) they provide an organization of knowledge not provided by an alternative system (note that uniqueness of a flow-chart).

A Third Order Interaction

Equipped with these theoretical arguments and empirical evidence it is obvious that audio-visual media, when examined through their symbol systems, serve as good or poor conveyors of information in interactions with learners' aptitudes and specific modes of internal representation. But it is also warranted to argue that, apart from the above, media's symbol systems, which can cultivate cognition, enter into another far more pervasive interaction with learners. We tend often to speak of learners as rather passive recipients of knowledge and as clay-like subjects whose skills are being molded. But once we entertain the possibility that they do something *active* with the skills they acquire and particularly with the symbolic codes they internalize from the media, we will have to look at them as individuals who actively gather information and structure it in terms of what they have acquired.

Thus, to quote Bowers (1973): 'The situation is a function of the observer in the sense that the observer's cognitive schemes filter and organize the environment in a fashion that makes it impossible ever to completely separate the environment from the person observing it' (pp. 328-329).

The learner who has internalized the filmic code of, say, changing spatial points of view into his/her imagery can now turn to his/her world of experience and represent it in ways that he/she was less able to do before. Here is the testimony of a student:

> "I am fascinated by how my daydreaming is influenced by movies. Processes and techniques of presenting events by this Hollywood symbol system are powerfully implanted within my cognitive system. I have observed third person narration, flashbacks, zooms, slow-motion emphasis of action, audience viewing, re-takes, 'voice of conscience', multi-personality dialogue, background music, and many other movie means of expression in my head. I fear that there is very little original style to my daydreaming. It is all influenced by celluloid... There are scenes where I am climbing steps to address a large audience, and television shots in slow motion symbolize the slow and hard road to significant others and flashbacks to significant moments."

While that student seems to be using filmic structures, in a representational capacity, it would make sense to hypothesize that he also examines other people's behaviour in similar terms. His mental, film-like schemata guide his perception and understanding of the world. This we call a *third order interaction.*

It can be imagined as a spiral in which one's mental apparatus guides perception and interpretation, which in turn establishes contact with new symbolic forms. The latter can be internalized, and when they are—they enrich the mental apparatus.

It is a justification for audio-visual usage because we want our students to use rich and alternative modes of internal representations, not just the verbal one, and we want them to examine the world through more than one symbol system. After all, insights of many scientists did not start with propositions. On the contrary, it was imagery—often adapted from the world of art—which served as the initial key hole through which phenomena were examined (see Shepard, 1978, for a compendium of such instances in the history of science).

But such third order interactions, whose nature we know only in skeletal form, need also to serve as a focus for research. We know too little which symbol systems are, or can be internalized, how they guide thinking and perception and how the latter are externalized for communication purposes.

From the above mentioned discussion it becomes obvious that visual media can be more emphatic in teaching-learning process. Keeping in view the utility of visual media, modern libraries are equipping themselves with such aids in digital collection.

4

Modern Librarianship and Information Science

> "All progress and growth is a matter of change, but change must be growth within our social and government concepts if it should not destroy them."
>
> —*Herbert Hoover*

As is conventionally understood, libraries are the repositories of knowledge. From the beginning days to modern era of information, libraries have traversed a chequered path. Similar is the case with library professionals. Modern day librarian is not only a professional but a information scientists also.

In the present chapter we shall elucidate this theme in pros and cons.

From the preceding chapters it can be seen that libraries have always endeavored to serve the needs of the societies of which they were a part. As the needs of these societies increased and changed, libraries, too, changed—in the number and forms of materials acquired, the methods of organizing and making them accessible, the number and kinds of services offered, and the kinds of facilities and equipment provided. Admittedly, change in library practices has often been slow, seldom—if ever—dramatic, reluctant in most instances, and too late in some cases, with the result that some other agency, institution, or professional group has taken over.

To Electronic Digital Computer

It is pertinent to note here that since the early 1940s, the increasing value and use of information as a commodity demanded the development of faster and more efficient facilities and processes for identifying collecting, and analyzing, evaluating, and disseminating it. Beginning in government and industry, where the need first presented itself to organize more specifically and speedily the recorded information of a narrowly defined subject field in support of intensive scientific research, the need has now spread to all disciplines.

During the past decades, emphasis on the importance of information as vital to economic and national development has resulted in the proliferation of information services: databases, bibliographic utilities, information professionals (translators, indexers, abstractors, managers, etc.) utilizing an increasing number of electronic devices, notably the computer and computer-like technologies. There is general agreement that the electronic digital computer is the most versatile and helpful of all the machines, instruments and devices which have been produced to assist humans in carrying out important tasks.

The multiple demonstrated capacities of the computer and its assumed potentials are so highly regarded that the "age of automation" is usually thought of as dating from the time when the first of these electronic devices, ENIAC, was switched on in 1946 at the Armcy Proving Grounds in Aberdeen, Maryland, for the purpose of providing high-speed computational assistance in the national defense program. Discovery of new uses for the computer and auxiliary machines has continued steadily since that time and today few, if any, areas of life have been left untouched by these machines.

Along with the development of new uses, there has come a steady improvement in the performance and capabilities of computers in their calculating speed, storage capacity or memory, compactness and flexibility, and economy of operation. Over the years, various technologies have offered libraries more efficient ways of acquiring, organizing, storing, and/ or transmitting information and knowledge, including the telephone, typewriter, paper tape, punched cards, copy machine, microforms, audio, visual, and audiovisual forms.

It is apt to note here that introduction of the computer into library operations has come slowly. The repretivie and routine library tasks have yielded most readily to mechanization. Computers have proved most useful in such traditional operations as the acquisition of materials: the performance of bookkeeping, payroll, and accounting work; maintaining in ventories of supplies and equipment; developing and updating patron registration files; preparing catalogs; recording circulation; expediting serials work; and keeping track of faculty reading and research interests. In the early 1960s, the Library of Congress began to study the possibility of using computer technology in the cataloging of library materials. By 1966, a pilot program was initiated for the distribution of cataloging data in machine-readable form to selected libraries. From this pilot program, Machine Readable Cataloging (MARC), has come computerized cataloging, the establishment of cooperative cataloging databses, and bibliographic utilities such as OCLC and

RLIN, and the online public access catalog now in widespread use. Even with the success of MARC, utilization of the computer in the storage and retrieval of information did not come easily or quickly to libraries. Lack of trained staff, patron and staff resistance to machines, unwillingness to change from established and familiar practices and formats to something "new and strange", inadequate space, inconvenience, the time required for the change, and the high cost of electronic equipment encouraged opposition.

However, many factors influenced the adoption of the computer in libraries: the attention given to the new technologies—notably the computer—in library schools and in library and information science literature during the past decade; increasing familiarity with the computer in daily life; the proven capabilities of the computer and other electronic devices in performing library functions; additional funding from state and federal governments and industry for advanced technological equipment and training; pressure from administrators, patrons, and staff; availability of more trained personnel; competition from nonlibrary agencies; development of more economical microcomputers; availability of integrated systems; and perhaps lastly, acceptance of the inevitable.

Now, more and more libraries are finding the computer a necessary tools with unlimited potential for performing library operations.

A major function of librarianship has always been to organize whatever types of materials have been available at the time; to recover, find, or retrieve information and knolwedge from these materials; and utilizing any and all available methods, to transmit them in some usable form to those needing or requesting them. However, when librarianship was not ready or able to satisfy *all* the additional needs involved in managing the tremendous volume of information, a new discipline began to emerge.

First called information retrieval, then documentation, it is now known as information science. There is no consensus regarding a defintion of information science, but there is agreement about what it does. According to the American Society for Information Science (ASIS), information science brings together and uses the theories, principles, techniques, and technologies of a variety of disciplines in solving information problems including computer science psychology, mathematics, logic, information theory, electronics, communication, linguistics, classification science, library science, management science, and economics. In the broadest sense, the basic objectives of librarianship and information science are the same. Both are concerend with the acquistion, storing, and retrieval of information for use.

However, there are major difference of emphasis in the techniques employed, especially the emphasis of information science on the use of computers and other electronic devices and on the interdisciplinary foundations of information science.

In addition, library science is associated with a specific institution, the library, while information science is concerned with the creation, storage, retrieval and dissemination of information independent of any specific environment. With the growing volume of information, librarians and library educators became increasingly aware of the need to find more efficient and rapid ways of managing it.

In 1950, Ralph Shaw, head of the U.S. Department of Agriculture Library developed the Rapid Selector, a complex device designed for searching recorded information, using electronics, optics, and photography. The Center for

Documentation and Communication Research was established at Case Western Reserve University in 1955—the first information science research organization to be located in a university library school. Emphasis was on bibliographic organization, information storage and retrieval, indexing, and abstracting as they related to librarianship.

Remarkably, various experiments in informations transfer were undertaken during the 1960s. An example was INTREX (Information Transfer Experiment) at MIT, a project directed toward the development of new methods for handling technical and scientific information, utilizng an online computer-based complex of devices easily accessible to users. In 1966, the Library of Congress began the distribution of cataloging data in machine readable form to selected libraries. By the 1960s, library schools began to add the word information to their title and offered courses in areas of information science, such as computer programming and library systems analysis.

Then, as now, in many instances new courses were devoted chiefly to some aspect of the computer and its use in libraries with little, if any, attention given to the science of information. Information science is not computer science. The focus of computer science is on computer programming, data processing, and mathematics. Information science, as stated above, is concerned with solving information problems using the technologies of various disciplines, computer science being only one.

It is also concerned with the nature of information—its generation, organization, processing, and distribution, and with all information activities. Information activities include many traditional library functions: collecting, classifying, recording, storing, providing bibliographic and physical access to information through reference service and, more recently, oneline bibliographic and databse searching.

Other information activities, some of which are carried on in special, research, and large public and university libraries include interpreting, analyzing, evaluating, translating, abstracting, indexing, and creating information. Still others involve teaching information professionals and developing and marketing information products. The emergence of many occupational groups concerned with the organization and dissemination of information and knowledge has given rise to dire predictions about the future of the library, e.g., "the library as an institution housing a physical collection" will eventually become obsolete and print on paper will be replaced by electronic publication. Some persns believe that the basic function of the library will not change as we move into the electronic environment, but that the ways in which these functions are carried out will change.

Others feel that to date no technology has replaced the printed word, but suggest that the usefulness of the printed page may not last. In the preceding chapters, it has been shown that many libraries have adopted new technologies, such as the computer, videcassettes, CD-ROM, and various forms of telecommunications and are utilizing them in library operations in their efforts to provide better service for their clienteles.

Most libraries are in various stages of introducing and/or adopting some of the electronic technologies for the same purpose. In state, public, school, academic, special, and research libraries, the influences of the information age are apparent in their standards, operations, services, planning, and cooperative arrangements.

Library schools are accepting the responsibility for preparing librarians/information professionals who can perform in many different information environments by designing curricular offerings which include such interdisciplinary offerings as library science/management, library science/communication, library science/business, and library science/computer science.

Education and Training

Remarkably, volume and complexity of information and the continuing development of more and more sophisticated electronic means of managing it have created the need for persons devoted to studying and understanding all of the activities involved in producing, acquiring, processing, analyzing, evaluating, and distributing this information. The educations and training of information professionals is a growing concern of schools of library and information science education and considerable attention is given in the literature and in numerous conferences, meeting, and seminars to designing course and model curricula. Attention is also being directed to identifying the skills and competencies which information professionals should have.

Some of these competencies are considered basic in librarianship, such as subjecte specializations, ability to use materials and technology, and skills related to each speciic activity performed in the library. Information workers should also have a knowledge of the structure and format of information; of the individuals, organizations, and institutions constituting the information environment, of what is required to provide service and produce products; and of what services and products are needed.

In addition to a thorough grounding in library science, the information professional should have a background of study in certain disciplines, such as philosophy, linguistics, mathematics, and/or the social and behavioral sciences.

It is pertinent to note that education and training of information professionals are provided by library schools whose graduates are employed in numerous information environments other than libraries; by other schools and divisions in colleges and universities, such as colleges of business or engineering whose graduates work with computers; in accounting, and in various aspects of information management; and by government agencies and industry.

The professional organization for information professionals is the American Society for Infromation Science (ASIS). Founded in 1937 as the American Documentation Institute, its initial interest was in the development of microfilm. In 1968, the name was changed to American Society for Information Science emphasizing its members concern with all aspects of the information-transfer process.

ASIS defines its purposes as "the provision of knowledge, leadership and development opportunities for information professionals and organizations to enhance and advance the state of the art of information science and its applications"

It provides a variety of services to its members, including conferences, meetings, continuing education programs, and publications. Among its 4000 members are information specialists from such fields as computer science, enginerring, management, linguistics, librarianship, and education.

Other professional associatiosn concerend with information activities are the American Library Association, Special Libraries Association, and Association for Library and Information Science Education. The National Commission on Library and Information Science has the responsibility for developing and recommending plans for meeting the library and information needs of the people of the United States.

Additional contributions to information science have been made by the federal government , the National Science Foundation, the Council on Library Resources, and industry through grants and other financial support to further research in specirfic areas.

A growing body of materials—textbooks, monograph, journals, conference proceedings, dictionaries, encyclopedias, audio, visual, and audiovisual materials research reports, etc.—produced, by the various groups concerned with information—keep the formation professional up-to-date.

Thus it becomes obvious from the foregoing discussion that the profession of library science has become hi-tech. Well trained professionals in the field are in great demand. To meet the challenges librarians have to master themselves in current and upcoming technology.

5

Library Reference Sources and Computer Searches

Success in doing research is largely a matter of combining knowledge of techniques, knowledge of sources and persistence. Researchers initiating inquiries will want to be aware of specialized encyclopaedias and state-of-the-art review articles and then of the several techniques that can be used to find more in-depth information:

- Controlled vocabulary subject heading searches in manual indexes.
- Systematic browsing.
- Key word searches in manual indexes.
- Citation searches in manual indexes.
- Searches using published bibliographies.
- Computer searches (which can be done via subject headings, key words, or citations, but add the possibility [among other advantages] of post-coordinate Boolean combinations while [among other limitations] diminishing the possibilities of browsing).
- Talking to knowledgeable people.

Each of these seven methods is potentially applicable

in any subject area; each has distinct advantages and disadvantages; and each is capable of turning up information that cannot be reached by the other six. It is also advisable to remember that all computer searches have noteworthy limitations, that Boolean combinations of subjects can be accomplished by both online and noncomputer methods and that particular treasures lie in special collections, government documents and microform collections—which must be sought out more actively than other sources.

A knowledge of these few distinct techniques—and of the advantages and limitations of each—will enable most researchers to substantially increase the range and efficiency of their investigations in any subject area. Most scholars, unfortunately, do most of their research only on the basis of (1) looking at footnotes in sources they already have, (2) inefficient use of card catalogues and (3) general browsing in the classified bookstacks of libraries. Those in the sciences tend to minimize even these pursuits, relying instead on taking to acquaintances. Very few researchers use catalogues and indexes efficiently because they routinely look under the wrong terms (confusing titles with subject headings or looking under generic rather than specific headings) and because they are familiar with only a small fraction of the range of indexes that exist. Reference to the outline of procedures sketched above, however, will enable most researchers to gain a simple overview of the *full range of options* available to them in any inquiry and (I hope) also assist them to achieve a sense of "closure" in making estimates of what research remains to be done.

A knowledge of techniques, however, must be supplemented by a knowledge of sources. And this is facilitated by an understanding that the finding aids and reference materials in any field predictably tend to fall into certain *types* of publications that collectively form a kind of structure within the literature. Here it is to be noted that by "reference materials" we mean those that either point the way into the core literature contained in journals, reports, monographs, dissertations, etc.; or those that summarize, abstract, digest, or review it. Reference materials tend to be those forms of literature that are simply consulted rather than read from cover to cover.

A foreknowledge of this overall structure can alert you to distribute your efforts among a variety of paths of inquiry; it can also give you a sense of what further options are available if your initial attempts are unsuccessful in finding the desired information. The various "bones" within the reference structure are:

1. *Bibliographies.* These list publications on a particular subject, often including materials that are missed by online databases.
2. *Computer databases.* These often contain the same information as conventional indexes and abstracts, but they offer the advantage of allowing you to comb through it in different ways (*e.g.*, by key word searches and post-coordinate Boolean combinations).
3. *Indexes and abstracts.* These serve to get you to the journal articles and research reports on your subject. Abstracts have the added advantage of providing brief summaries of the items they index, which enable you to do a quick literature review at an early stage of your research.
4. *Encyclopaedias.* Here the specialized sets devoted to particular subject areas are often more useful than the widely known general sets. The purpose of an encyclopaedia is to summarize knowledge and to

provide a starting point for more extensive research; it seeks to present an overview of a subject written in such a way that a nonspecialist can understand it. (Note that sets specialized in a particular *subject area* still tend to be written with a nonspecialist *audience* in mind). An encyclopaedia may be contrasted to a *treatise,* which attempts to provide all knowledge on a subject in a systematic (rather than an alphabetical) arrangement and which may be written for specialists rather than laypeople.

5. *Guides to the literature.* These often provide a connected expository overview of the literature of a subject and its reference sources.

6. *Review articles.* State-of-the-art reviews are somewhat like encyclopaedia articles in attempting to provide an overall assessment of the state of knowledge of a particular subject. They are often longer, however; they are frequently written for an audience of specialists familiar with a particular jargon; and they often seek to provide comprehensive rather than simply introductory bibliographies.

7. *Directories.* These serve to lead you to people, organizations, or institutions that are interested in and knowledgeable about particular subjects. They are especially valuable because they often provide the best key to the tremendous stores of knowledge that exist outside libraries.

9. *Newsletters and loose-leaf services.* These provide daily or weekly updates of information in rapidly changing fields.

8. *Handbooks and Almanacs.* These serve as compendia of a variety of miscellaneous information and are often especially good for tabular or statistical data.

10. *Union lists.* These enable you to identify which libraries own copies of the particular publications you are seeking.
11. *Yearbooks.* These provide reviews and assessments of the most recent year's developments in a field.

Remarkably, within several of these categories it is useful to distinguish further which sources are searchable by subject headings, by key words, or by classified subject-grouping arrangement. The *method* of searching involved will have a significant effect on the results that can be achieved. Students within a particular discipline usually learn its reference sources from a particular list they are given to study. The result is that they often learn the individual trees very well without perceiving the arrangement of the forest or the variety of methods available for getting through it, whether by walking, riding, flying over, swinging from branch to branch, or burrowing underneath. The training of reference librarians, on the other hand, is more from the top down than from the bottom up. They learn first the overall arrangement that can be expected in *any* forest—here the analogy is not perfect—and the various methods of moving around in it.

They hold an overall set of *categories* of sources in mind, with a knowledge of several distinct methods of combing each category (*e.g.*, "What this question requires is a bibliography arranged by a subject classification scheme rather than alphabetically by subject headings"; "What this question demands is an index that allows a key word approach rather than subject heading access"; "What this question requires is a database that allows citation searching coupled with post-coordinate limitations by key words").

Even though they may not know particular titles or

file names within a subject area, they do know beforehand that they can *reasonably expect* to find certain *types* of sources within which they can *reasonably expect* to find certain *methods* of access available, each with its own advantages and disadvantages. They therefore usually understand the *full range of options* for finding information even on unfamiliar subjects; for this reason they can often provide material on a subject more efficiently than even full professors within the discipline.

The librarians may not understand the content of the discipline; but they do understand the predictable systems and methods of *finding* the content, which is a distinct matter. And the study of what can be expected in the arrangement, categorization, storage and retrieval of information is a discipline unto itself: it is called library and information science.

Those who have not studied it formally should be very careful about assuming that they are doing fully efficient research "on their own", for there will almost always be more options in searching than they realize. The moral of the story is brief: the more you know of what your options are, the better the searcher you will be; but remember to ask for help because the probability is that you will miss something important if you work entirely on your own.

Basically, librarians have three major aids that help them to exploit the internal structure of the information sources within any given field. The first can be considered the basic source; the other two, updates. They are:

1. *Guide to Reference Books,* edited by Eugene Sheehy (10th ed.; American Library Association, 1986). This volume, known as "Sheehy", is the reference librarian's bible. It enables a searcher to look up

any subject field and find within it a definitive listing of virtually all its important reference sources arranged according to the types of literature. The citations provide full bibliographic descriptions of each source for exact identification, plus descriptive annotations. The overall arrangement of the volume is by broad subject groups, with an index by authors, title and subjects.

2. *Reference Sources* (Pierian Press, 1977). This annual publication is a comprehensive list of reference sources in all fields published during the year. Beginning with the 1980 volume it is arranged alphabetically by LC subject headings, with indexes by author and title. It is most useful as an ongoing and regular update of the latest Sheehy edition.
3. *ARBA: American Reference Books Annual,* edited by Bohdan S. Wynar (Libraries Unlimited, Inc., 1970). Each annual volume in this series presents a listing of all reference books published in the United States within the preceding year. The distinctive feature of the series is that it provides a detailed review of each work listed. Indexes are by author, title and subject. *ARBA* thus serves as another excellent update of Sheehy. Three five-year cumulative indexes (1970-1974, 1975-1979 and 1980-1984) have appeared since the beginning of the series and these cumulations are themselves major guides to reference books. Some libraries keep them next to their Sheehy.

There is still another volume—a kind of "mini-Sheehy" —that every researcher should own. This is *Reference Books: A Brief Guide,* compiled by Marion V. Bell and Eleanor A.

Swidan (Enoch Pratt Free Library, revised irregularly). It is an excellent brief list, with comparative and evaluative annotations, of the most important reference sources in all fields. Ordering information can be found in *Paperbound Books in Print.*

Computer Searches

Practically, Computer searches offer a convenient way to generate a bibliography on virtually any subject a researcher may be interested in and they can provide other information as well.

Basically, there are four kinds of online searches and they should not be confused with each other:

1. OCLC-type searches, which serve as book or journal location devices (*i.e.*, they can tell you which libraries in the country own a copy of the work you are seeking).
2. Searches through commercial systems (*e.g.*, Dialog, SDC, BRS) that produce printouts of bibliographic citations on any subject, often with abstracts.
3. Searches using the online catalogues of particular libraries, which provide bibliographic citations to some materials (usually only recent books) held by those institutions.
4. Full-text searches, available through commercial systems, which retrieve whole articles, reports, or tabular data rather than just citations to them.

It is pertinnet to note that are so many developments in the computer field and they are happening so quickly, that only a fool would try to present a coherent overview of the situation.

OCLC-Type Searches

OCLC, Inc., is a shared-cataloging network with about 3800 participating libraries, with an additional 2500 adjunct members, in all 50 states, Canada and several other countries. It is remarkable that initials used to stand for "Ohio College Library Center"; but now, under different management, it is the "Online Computer Library Center". Before the advent of this system (and others like it), individual libraries each had to do a considerable amount of original cataloging of new books to create catalogue cards and other records of their holdings.

Now, a library can find out if any other library in the system has already cataloged a particular book and use that information in the computer to generate the needed records for local use at the push of a button. Participants in the system do not have to individually re-invent the wheel for every new book, in other words. The process of simplifying the task of cataloging produces a spinoff benefit: whenever a library uses the stored cataloging information on a particular book or journal, that library is automaticaily recorded by the system as owning that item.

Searchers may therefore request the cataloging data on a book and then see a list of libraries that actually own a copy of the volume. The operation started in 1967 but did not really attract a lot of members until the early 1970s and so the database contains only records of works cataloged after these dates. Some libraries are going back and entering their earlier holdings into the system; but this is a very expensive operation and, under the present economic circumstances, there is little incentive to recatalog works for which they already have the necessary records, albeit in manual form. Still, there are hundreds of thousands of pre-1970 works in the database because even though they may have been published 50—or 350—years ago, they were not acquired and cataloged by a library until the last few years.

And the date of the book's being cataloged, not that of its publication, determines its presence or absence in the database. Currently, the system records locations for about eleven million items, about a third of which were published prior to the 1960s.

Records in OCLC cannot be searched by subject—you must already know the author or the title of a work in order to find it. There are two other networks in the United States that compete with OCLC. These are the Research Libraries Information Network (RLIN) and the Washington Library Network (WLN). (A third system, UTLAS, links Canadian libraries but is seeking customers in the states as well). RLIN includes several big-name libraries such as the New York Public, Yale, Princeton, Columbia and Stanford; WLN is made up of libraries mainly in the Pacific Northwest. If a desired item cannot be located through an OCLC search, or through the several other sources, a search of RLIN or WLN may still turn up a copy.

The RLIN database has an especially important feature: it is in the process of assembling catalogue records, with library locations, for all works published anywhere in the entire British Empire in the eighteenth century, plus all works in English published anywhere else in the world for the same century. This is known as the Eighteenth Century Short Title Catalogue project and a huge set of microfiche of all the significant works identified in the project is also being produced.

Commercial Bibliographic Databases

Three major vendor companies provide the computer

search services to which most libraries subscribe: Dialog Information Services, Inc. (a subsidiary of Lockheed Corp)., System Development Corporation (or SDC, which offers a search service known as ORBIT) and Bibliographic Retrieval Services (or BRS). A fourth source, the National Library of Medicine, offers its own MEDLARS system to subscribers; this is confined to medical and related subject areas, however. The other three companies offer over 250 different databases. Each such database is a file of information (usually bibliographic citations to journal articles or research reports) in a particular subject area, stored in machine-readable form.

There is considerable overlap in the files offered by the various vendors (*e.g.*, the *Psychological Abstracts* database is offered by all three), but the broadest range is provided by Dialog. When the librarian or other trained searcher uses a local terminal connected via telephone line to the vendor's computer, he or she can interact with the machine to tailor the search to particular subjects or combinations of subjects.

The methods of instructing the computer vary to some extent depending on which vendor's system is being used. A computer search enables you to scan thousands of citations to journal articles in virtually any subject area. The result, in most cases, will be a printed bibliography tailored to your specific requirements; in some subject areas you have the option of receiving abstracts of the articles.

Most searches done at academic libraries for students or other university personnel will probably cost between $5 and $30 for each database searched; this wiil include charges for the amount of computer and teleconnect time and for the number of citations actually retrieved. There may also be a surcharge for service levied by the individual library. Those who are not affiliated with a university can obtain searches through private research companies, through some local public libraries, or, sometimes, through joining a university library's "Friends of the Library" organization. Two good directories that list facilities that will do searches for you are the *Online Database Search Services Directory* (Gale Research) or any edition of *American Library Directory* after 1982.

It is noteworthy that bibliography created by the computer will be mailed to the requesting library or search service and received about a week after the search is run; it can also be printed immediately at the local terminal if instant results are required, but this costs more in computer time and teleconnect fees. Most people wait for mail delivery if the printout will be lengthy. The librarian or other searcher must select in advance which of the 250 + databases she wishes to search for your subject and for some topics she may have to use several files. There is no way to search all of the databases simultaneously. The Dialog system, however, offers a separate "Dialindex" database that can efficiently point out which of the many files will yield results for a particular search statement. SDC and BRS have somewhat similar features.

People who request computer searches are well advised to be aware that many databases are in a one-to-one correspondence with a conventional printed index. The *Sociological Abstracts* computer file, for example, contains exactly the same information that can be found in the printed index of the same name. The education database, called *ERIC*, contains the same information as the printed version; similarly, *Historical Abstracts* corresponds to its printed form, *Philosopher's Index* to its and so on. The reason for this is that the computer companies simply acquire the magnetic tapes from which the printed indexes are originally generated and mount them in a way that allows for direct searching.

In many cases, then, researchers who inquire about online services find that they really do not need them and that a half hour spent with the print indexes is quite sufficient. Often there are significant differences between the databases and the print indexes, however. In most instances only the comparatively recent years of an index are searchable online. The hard copy version of *Biological Abstracts,* for example, covers from 1927 to date; but only the years 1969 to the present are in the database. Similarly, the print index *Public Affairs Information Service (P.A.I.S).* covers from 1915 to date; but only the years from 1976 are loaded in the computer. *Psychological Abstracts* is searchable online from 1967 onwards; but the hard copy version extends back to 1927. There may be other differences as well. One can search titles and abstracts of doctoral dissertations via computer from June 1980 to date; but prior to that time one can search only their titles and not their abstracts, which were not put into the database.

To search the abstracts, one must use the printed *Dissertation Abstracts.* Similarly, even though the *Biological Abstracts* database covers from 1969 to date, none of the entries from 1969 through June 1976 includes an abstract. The scope of coverage (as well as the dates) may also vary between print and online versions. Since May 1980 the *Psychological Abstracts* database has included about 25% *more* material (mainly doctoral dissertations) than is found in the print version. And, on the other side of the coin, the computer files corresponding to the *Science* and *Social Sciences Citation Indexes,* for several years of coverage, have *less* material than their printed counterparts:

- The hard copy *Science Citation Index* (1955—) covers conference proceedings and multiauthored books and *Festschriften* (indexed at the chapter or essay level) for five years, 1977—1981, in addition to its coverage of journal articles and "Annual Review" type publications. But the corresponding *Scisearch* database (1974—) includes only the latter forms—not the conference proceedings or multiauthored books. But as of 1982 the two are essentially the same again (neither covering the proceedings or multiauthored books), although *Scisearch* covers *Current Contents,* which the print version does not.
- The hard copy *Social Sciences Citation Index* (1966—) covers multiauthored anthologies indexed at the chapter or essay level, in addition to journals, for the years 1979—1982. It also covers conference proceedings for the three years 1979— 1981. The *Social Scisearch* database (1972—), however, covers only journals.

As might be expected, there are both advantages and disadvantages in having a computer search done rather than using the print indexes. There are several advantages:

1. The computer can save your time in searching. When you use print indexes, you have to repeat the same search over and over again through many annual volumes and monthly supplements—some of which may be missing from the shelf in your particular library. But the machine can search all the information within a database all at once.

2. The computer may be slightly more up-to-date than the print index. The newest "issue" of an index may be

loaded online days or even weeks before the print version appears on the library's shelves.

3. In addition to searching subject headings, the computer can search for key words within titles or even abstracts. This is an extremely important advantage, especially in those files for which the print version allows access only through a controlled-vocabulary system. *Psychological Abstracts,* for instance, has its own controlled-vocabulary list of subject headings, so you must find a relevant term from this list in order to gain subject access to the printed version of the index. This can be a problem if there is no term in the list that corresponds to what you want. To return to a previous example, a researcher at the time of 'the Iranian hostage crisis had trouble in this regard, since in 1980 there were no subject headings using the words "Hostage", "Captive", "Terrorism", or "Kidnap"; nor were variants such as "Captivity" or "Terrorist" used. Nor were there any cross-references from these words to other terms that were acceptable to the system. In using the print index, then, he was stymied. But in having a computer search done he circumvented the difficulty because the machine was able to examine the same file of information for *any* word appearing in either the titles or the abstracts; and a search on the terms "hostage?" or "terror?" 1 produced a large list of directly relevant articles. (The records on a computer printout have a "descriptor field" analogous to the subject tracings on a catalogue card, which told the searcher in this case that the articles did indeed appear in the print index— under the headings 'Violence" and "Crime victims"). Similarly, a few years ago the same *Psychological Abstracts* thesaurus did not have the term "Burnout" as either a heading or a cross-reference; but a computer search under the term as a key word produced a bibliography of over two hundred items. And here the descriptor fields

indicated that the articles were scattered under several subject headings in the print index (e.g., "Employee attitudes", "Occupational adjustment", "Occupational aspirations", "Occupational stress"). Here, a key word approach was clearly more efficient than that afforded by subject headings.

Academic researchers in the fields of language, literature and linguistics should especially note that the Modern Language Association's *MLA International Bibliography* is searchable online, although at present only from the 1960s to date. (The entire index from 1921 'nill eventually be entered into the database). The print version of this index, prior to 1981, is notoriously difficult to search for subjects other than particular authors and their works. The computer, however, now provides key word access to any terms within the titles of books or articles.

4. In some databases the machine can also do other types of searches that are not possible with the printed indexes, such as searching by document type. In the general *Scisearch* and *Social Scisearch* files, for example, one can search directly for state-of-the-art review articles. And many of the other databases that are more comprehensive in specialized fields (*e.g., PSYCHINFO, ERIC, MEDLINE)* have similar features that can pull out review articles, or letters to the editor, or book reviews, curriculum guides and so on.

5. Another major advantage of a computer search is its ability to look for two or more subject terms at the same time. For example, if you are interested in "Fungal diseases in conifers in Canadian forests", in a printed index you would have to look under at least three different headings (fungal diseases, conifers, Canada) separately and then weed out all the articles that don't appear under each of

the three. But the computer can search all three subjects simultaneously and give you only the citations that meet all three specifications. This combining or crossing capability is particularly useful where each separate idea is itself expressable in several variant phrasings.

A search of the corresponding printed *ERIC* indexes under all nine headings would have been very time consuming. The computer, however, could search for all four of the first-column terms at once and all five of the second column and then cross the two sets against each other, printing only those citations that "hit" at least one descriptor from each column simultaneously. Had he so desired, the searcher could have introduced a third column, limiting the output to only those citations indexed under the descriptors "Secondary schools", "Secondary education", "Secondary school curriculum" and so on. A further specification could have produced a final set composed only of those relevant articles published in the last five years.

The computer accomplishes this process of combining and screening through operations of "Boolean logic", which can be illustrated in Figure 6(Q). If Circle A represents the set of citations retrieved by terms expressing one subject idea (either controlled-vocabulary descriptors or key words or both) and Circle B represents another subject, then the area of overlap represents those citations that deal with both subjects. Other circles or limiting factors can be introduced for further specification. And other types of combinations are possible, as shown in Figure 6(b) and 6(c).

The combination of these five factors frequently makes computer searching a highly useful technique. There are, however, some limitations to its usefulness; and there are positive disadvantages as well:

1. A computer search costs money and the bibliography it generates takes time to arrive. Usually the printout will be received in less than a week; but it still takes a matter of days. (Those researchers who want an instant printout can obtain it at the local terminal, but this will cost more). For brief or uncomplicated searches, the use of print indexes rather than their online versions can thus save both time and money.

2. Contrary to the naive assumption held by many people, the computer cannot tap into "all knowledge". Nor can it search all of its 250 + databases simultaneously—each must be selected and entered separately. Moreover, the vocabulary used to search one file may not work in the others—the subject terms may have to be tailored to each. And without such careful tailoring you may miss the best material.

3. The databases are mainly good for picking up journal articles and research reports. Some of them, particularly within the last few years, are picking up books, too—but the problem is that you cannot *count* on them to have picked up all relevant monographs. The various producers of the files publish lists of the journals they index; but they don't do this for books, nor do they clearly specify the criteria by which they select books. A further problem relates to the depth of indexing done on monographs—do they index the contents of individual chapters? Or of the book as a whole? Or just title key words? The indexing procedures are seldom clear.

4. The number of descriptors or subject headings assigned to each article may vary greatly from one database to the

next. *Historical Abstracts* averages 3.6 per article; *Psychological Abstracts,* 6; and *NTIS* (National Technical Information Service) between 8 and 24. The number of these assigned points of access determines how readily the information can be retrieved and how successfully Boolean combinations will work. And even in those databases in which access is only through key words, the number of words available for each item determines its accessibility—that is, if you can search only titles, you cannot retrieve as many items as you could if abstracts were also searchable. Most dissertations, for example, are retrievable only through title key words, since abstracts are not in the database prior to June 1980.

The type of problem this results in is illustrated by the student of English literature who wishes to compile a list of all doctoral dissertations on the Romantic critic and essayist William Hazlitt. A computer search on "Hazlitt?" in the *Dissertation Abstracts* database turns up over 50 items—but it also misses *at least a dozen* other dissertations having substantial sections on the essayist. The reason is that these extra items pre-date 1980 and do not use the essayist's name in their titles, among which are *The Romantic Critics' Opinions of Elizabethan Non-Dramatic Literature* and *English Prose of the Romantic Age: The Matter of Style.*

5. Another related problem has to do with the difficulty of thinking up all synonyms and variant phrasings for a subject.

6. As noted above, most of the databases contain citations only from about the late 1960s or early 1970s, while the corresponding print indexes may cover many decades. When librarians point this out to students, however, the response we get is almost invariably, "Oh well, I need only the most recent material anyway". The facile assumption implied

here is that the most recent material will always cite or recapitulate anything of value from the older material. But there is a good chance that it won't—especially since many recent articles have themselves been researched solely on the basis of other computer searches. It is very easy for a vicious circle to develop—one in which researchers unwittingly rely too heavily on recent sources that have themselves relied too heavily on only recent sources. Human thought and scholarship did not begin only in the late 1960s.

You must be careful not to let your research be shaped too much by the simple convenience of one particular tool of research; the material that is most easily retrievable is not necessarily or automatically the best, most insightful, or most important.

7. When you have a computer search done, you are to some extent relinquishing to another person the responsibility for your research. And you have no guarantee that the searcher will do everything that you would want. For example, I was once asked to do a search for a graduate student in sociology on the topic "blended families" or "stepfamilies" (*i.e.*, those in which a parent remarries, resulting in a new family with stepchildren and a stepparent). The student assured me that she was already familiar with much of the literature, that she had checked through several annual volumes of the print indexes and that she was sure that these two terms were the only ones being used. I therefore did a search using these terms, in three databases and I came up with fifteen items. But I also noticed that the abstracts of some of the citations were using the term "reconstituted families". And so I went back and searched the three files again using this new term and I found *nineteen additional* items that had not been retrieved in the first search.

The question is obvious: what would have happened if I hadn't noticed the additional term? The answer is that the student would have missed more than half of the works she wanted to see—and she probably would never have known it. Since most people are very naive about what a computer printout actually covers, it is likely that she would have assumed that she had "everything" on her subject.

How often are searchers guilty of such potential omissions? It's hard to say because the only mistakes we can talk about are the ones we almost made, but caught. I suspect that if you had five different searchers look for information on the same subject, you would probably have as many different printouts. It is to be hoped that there would be considerable overlap in the results; but I would be surprised if the five were identical. Much depends on how successfully the searcher manages the initial interview with the requester and there is considerable room for variation here. In other words, one computer search is *by no means* necessarily as good as another—who does the search for you is a big factor in detennining *what* you will get for results. If you are associated with an academic institution, one good way to find out the names of the best searchers to ask the student assistants in the reference department. They usually know who is most capable.

8. Computer searches on key words are likely to produce some— or many—citations that have the right words in the wrong context. A search of the words "President" and "Washington" will turn up articles on George Washington—but also material on the President of Washington College. A search for material on the history of steamboats once turned up an article on the similarity of birth defects in five babies in Steamboat Springs, Colorado. *A* (bad) search that

was intended to retrieve articles on "how labor supply in an area affects managerial decisions on locating plants" crossed "labor" and "manag?" and unwittingly retrieved hundreds of articles on labor-management relations.

Computer searches thus have both advantages *and disadvantages.* To use them intelligently you must recognize their limitations as well as their strengths. The important thing to remember is that they are only one weapon available to the researcher; they are not the whole arsenal.

Online Library Catalogues

Many academic and public libraries are now making a change from card catalogues to computers. In most cases the switch involves closing the manual file and beginning the coverage of the database from that point forward—that is, the computer will usually not pick up retrospectively the material covered by the cards. In using an online catalogue, then, the first thing you must find out is its dates of coverage. It is *especially* important not to confuse the coverage of an online library catalogue with that of, say, a Dialog search. Commercial services such as Dialog include hundreds of databases that cover a very wide range of materials: books, journal articles, conference, papers, dissertations, government documents, research reports and newspaper articles.

An online catalogue search, however, is usually only *one* database of information on books—and only the books of the one library whose catalogue is being searched. It will not list "everything" in the library, in other words; and yet a surprising number of people seem to think that any "computer search" is just as good as any other and that "all knowledge" is somehow magically available through one-stop shopping at a library terminal. And what is just as frequent an occurrence is that even when librarians inform users of what is not covered by online catalogues, many of them still say that they will simply "settle for whatever is on the printout", as though the computer had automatically selected the best material. College students are the most frequent offenders in this regard; professors who expect high quality research should insist that their students use sources other than online catalogues alone. In most cases the contents of such a catalogue will be similar to that of the manual file it supersedes, that is, the individual items that can be searched will be the electronic equivalents of catalogue cards, each containing the name of a book's author, its title, call number and so on and two or three subject headings. What is likely to be different are the number of access points to the same information. With cards you can search by author, title, or approved subject heading; but with computers you may be able to search, in addition, by key words appearing anywhere on the record, by call number, by date of publication, by series, by language, or by any combination of such entries.

It used to be that libraries had to limit the number of access points in a manual catalogue to only a few because each additional point required the creation and filing of an entirely separate card (*e.g.*, if access by author is desired, one card for the book must be filed under the author's name; if access by two subject headings is desired, two separate cards must be created and filed). In a manual system, you cannot have access to a book under ten different subject headings without creating a very bulky and difficult-to-use file. But with a computerized record you can have as many points of access as you want because all of them are on *one* record, the creation of which entails neither the labor and expense of making and filing multiple copies of the record, nor the space problems of a physically bulky file.

Libraries now have the opportunity to create catalogue records that allow a much greater depth of access to information. Theoretically, the tables of contents or chapter headings of books can now be added to catalogue records to provide many more points of subject access; it is also now possible to add more than just the traditional two or three subject headings. Few libraries are making full use of the new opportunities, however; most follow the lead of the Library of Congress, which continues to create computerized records with not much more than the old-fashioned minimum of information on them.

The fact that online catalogues are very "high tech" and that, often, they will provide you with a *free* printout of results makes them very attractive research tools. Again, however, you must be on guard not to let the scope of your research be channelled too much in one direction by the fact that one tool is more visible or more attractive than others.

It is advisable to recall that an online catalogue will probably *not* cover such sources as:

(a) Individual chapters of books.

(b) Journal and magazine articles.

(c) Newspaper articles.

(d) State-of-the-art review articles.

(e) Nonbook formats such as prints, posters, photographs, motion pictures, sound recordings, sheet music, maps and manuscripts.

(f) Research reports such as those from the National

Technical Information Service (NTIS); or the Educational Resources Information Center (ERIC).

(g) U.S. government documents.

(h) Microform research collections.

In other words, even if you do a good search in an online catalogue, the likelihood is that you will be getting only the tip of the iceberg of what the library contains.

Full-Text Searches

Some companies offer databases that contain the full texts of newspaper or journal articles, court decisions, research reports and so on, rather than just citations to them. Pre-eminent among these is the Mead Corporation, which produces the LEXIS and NEXIS databases. LEXIS is a huge resource in the field of law; it contains the full text of the United States Code plus full decisions from the Supreme Court, Courts of Appeal, District Courts and Courts of Claims. It also provides specialized "libraries" in tax, securities, trade regulation, communications, labor, patent and copyright and other law-related subjects. NEXIS is a similarly huge database containing the full texts of all the stories in major newspapers and wire services for at least three years back, plus all articles from major magazines for at least the last five years. It includes full coverage of the *Washington Post, New York Times, Newsweek* and *U.S. News & World Report*—among dozens of other magazines—plus all Associated Press and United Press International releases.

The *Dow Jones News/Retrieval* service is another source of full-text material. It includes reports on individual companies, industries, stocks, bonds, financial matters in general and events in the news (including sports, movie reviews and weather reports).

Dialog is also getting more and more into the field of full-text databases. Among such files searchable on its system are:

- *Academic American Encyclopaedia,* which contains 30,000 articles and tables on all subjects, including material not found in the printed edition.
- *AP News,* which provides all stories from the Associated Press Data Stream service.
- *Commerce Business Daily,* which is the daily newsletter announcing and soliciting U.S. government contracts.
- *Harvard Business Review,* which provides the full text of the journal from 1976 to date, plus citations and abstracts for articles published from 1971 to 1975.
- *Magazine ASAP* and *Trade and Industry ASAP,* which provide complete texts of over 130 general and business magazines from January 1, 1983, to date.
- The full text of the King James version of the Bible.

Dialog offers over a dozen other full-text databases as well, primarily in the fields of business and current events. Others are planned for the future.

Despite the ongoing trend—indeed, rush—to put more full-text and tabular material online, it is worthwhile to remember that the bibliographic databases which provide only citations or abstracts rather than full texts will always allow you to do more extensive (although less in-depth) searches—and for a reason. Whenever a complete text is mounted, the database producer or vendor must have a licensing agreement with the owner of the copyright of the text. When citations *to* a text are offered, however, there are no copyright restrictions and so coverage can be much broader. These four different kinds of computer searches—book location, bibliographic citation, online library catalogue and full-text—are having an enormous impact on the way in which researchers operate. Especially valuable are their capabilities to search for key words in addition to subject headings and to do Boolean crossings of two or more subjects against each other. It should be noted, however, that computers are not the *only* means of finding such combinations of subjects.

The extended list includes:

1. *Computer searches.*
2. *The Permuterm Subject Index* volumes of ISI indexes, which enable you to search for combinations of any two key words appearing in the titles of journal articles.
3. *Precoordinated subject headings in conventional indexes and catalogues.* With a computer you can take two or more subjects that have not already been combined and cross them against each other to determine if there is any area of overlap; this is known as post-coordination of subjects. A *pre*coordinated heading, on the other hand, is one that in effect has already done such a combination for you; it already expresses in one phrase the overlap of two or more subjects, so you don't have to put them together yourself through post-coordinating computer manipulations.
4. *Standard subdivisions limiting headings in conventional indexes and catalogues.* Rather than expressing a relationship of one subject to another,

standard subdivisions were originally used to distinguish the various aspects that are *within* one subject. This distinction is usually nonexistent in actual cataloging practice, however. Their use constitutes another form of the precoordination of two or more terms.

There are hundreds of thousands of actual and potential precoordinated headings in any catalogue or index that uses the *LCSH* vocabulary system; some other controlled vocabularies have analogous capabilities. Reference librarians are trained, literally, *to think in these terms*—and researchers who wish to exploit collections in the same way are well advised to study the booklet *Library of Congress Subject Headings: A Guide to Subdivision Practice* (LC, 1981). To the extent that you understand the possibilities and probabilities that there may be a precoordinated heading for your subjects, you can in effect do Boolean limitations without a computer. This is an especially important skill to have if you need to do material too old to be in a database that allows for post-coordination. (Overzealous computer buffs sometimes tend to suggest that combinations of subjects can be found *only* with computers, as though it never occurred to anyone before about 1968 to want to put two or more ideas together. The standard subdivisions in the *LCSH* system, however, allow for surprising range and flexibility in this regard).

5. *Bibliographies with indexes.* This is sometimes the best way to cross ideas against each other. For example, a scholar looking for material comparing the philosophy of Sartre with that of Christianity

could turn to Franics H. Lapointe's *Jean-Paul Sartre and His Critics: An Annotated Bibliography* (1938—1980). He could then simply turn to its index to see which of the studies is listed under "Christianity". (There are eleven).

Even if a subject bibliography does not have an index, it is usually only a matter of a few moments to scan through its entries to look for relevant titles. "Combinations" can thus also be accomplished by systematic browsing in bibliographies. This is a good technique to remember because post-coordination via computers does not always work. (Again, remember that *nothing* works *all the time*—you must therefore have a variety of approaches at your disposal). *Published subject bibliographies are especially useful in allowing you to "cross" ideas in the older literature that is not picked up by databases.*

The versatility of computer searches is so dazzling that a large number of researchers are failing to note or heed their limitations. And, contrary to the popular saying, what you don't know *can* hurt you. I have seen this problem repeatedly, particularly with graduate students who want to do a literature review in preparation for writing a dissertation. One student, for example, told me that she'd heard that "there was a way to have all your research done for you automatically" and she wanted to know how to have that done. When I tried to explain to her how computer searches work and that they have certain limitations as to what they can provide, she did not want to listen. She wanted a printout that would give her everything, period and didn't care to hear otherwise. She finally said she'd "settle" for the computer search anyway, as she was "sure" it would give her enough for her dissertation (!) and, besides, she had a job and therefore "didn't have the time to do any other research". (This attitude is by no means atypical). Never mind that she was missing single-author books, or relevant chapters or discussions within books, on her subject; never mind that she was missing journal articles written before the early 1970s; never mind that she was searching only a few key words from only the titles of previous doctoral dissertations. Her casual assumption, as found in so many students, was that only "the most recent" material is worth reading and that the computer would give her she needed.

What is just as bad is that professors who direct doctoral dissertations *allow* computer searches to pass for complete literature reviews—for the professors are usually just as naive about their limitations as the students are. What this amounts to can only be described as cultural lobotomy on a grand scale. When a significant percentage of our most educated people (prospective Ph.Ds) relies almost exclusively on computer searches for "in-depth" research, then we are fostering the growth of an intellectual system with very shallow roots.

Since so much of the written memory of humanity before the 1970s is not in the computer in the first place—or is only superficially indexed—it is likely to be ignored by immature scholars if it isn't as easily retrievable as the more recent material. The older material—especially the older journal articles— "does not compute"; and to many graduate students this tends as a practical matter to mean "therefore it is not important". There tends to be a similar neglect of certain forms of literature, especially single-author books, because machines more readily retrieve journal articles and research reports.

A moment's reflection will indicate that the computers are no better than the material that is loaded into them; and yet a surprising number of researchers expect them to be omniscient.

Still, the *appropriate* use of computers is a boon of tremendous value to researchers. Two questions that must arise, then, are "How can I find out which databases exist in my subject area?" and "How can I find out what limitations there are in the coverage of these databases?" Several directories provide this information:

- *Data Base Directory* (Knowledge Industry Publications and the American Society for Information Sciences; irregular), which covers 1800 files with an index by subject.
- *Computer-Readable Databases: A Directory and Data Source-book* (Knowledge Industry Publications, for the American Society for Information Sciences; biennial) which covers over 700 databases, with a subject index.
- *Online Bibliographic Databases: A Directory and Source-book* (Gale Research; revised irregularly), which covers about 180 files.
- *Encyclopaedia of Information Systems and Services* (Gale Research; revised irregularly), which describes about 1500 databases and tells you whether the ones you want are available through the Dialog, SDC, or BRS systems, to which most libraries subscribe.
- *Datapro Complete Guide to Dial-Up Databases* (Datapro Research Corp)., a 600-page looseleaf directory of over 1400 databases with full descriptions and a subject index.

Computers, in short, are a very powerful resource for researchers—but they are only one among many and they are by no means always the best resource for particular inquiries. The major points to remember about computer searches are that they allow key word access to records otherwise available only through subject headings and that they allow for post-coordinate Boolean combinations of two or more different subjects. Beyond this, it is important to be aware that online searches do *not* provide access to "everything" and that, in fact, they have distinct *disadvantages as well as advantages*—and that their ability to combine subjects can sometimes be matched or superseded by other, conventional approaches.

6

Electronic Serials

Just as there are several terms for paper-based serials, so there are for the digital format: *electronic journals, online journals, digital journals* and the more all-embracing *electronic resources.* According to Thomas Nisonger, there is no standard accepted definition of an electronic journal serial.

E. journal is a reasonably short term and the one we will use, simply to save space. Producers take three broad approaches with e-journals: an electronic-only version of a new title, an electronic-only version of a title converted from a paper version and both an electronic and paper version. In the past decade or so, libraries and producers have struggled with how to migrate from a print-only world to one that is a mix of paper and electronic resources. The electronic side is becoming more and more dominant and will continue to do so in the future, at least in some serial categories. One of the first forays into the digital world that is still widely used is the CD-ROM product. Those first seen in libraries were primarily DOS-based and have since evolved to a Windows, environment. Starting principally with indexing and abstracting services, the CD-ROM products quickly became popular in reference departments. Proprietary software and differing search engines created and continue to create challenges for the library's public service staff. Stand-alone systems were satisfactory at first, but it was not long before there was signi-ficant pressure to "network" the stations and allow users to select from a number of products from any station.

Making CD "jukeboxes", network software, servers and user computers all work together is a continuing challenge for libraries. When the producers moved into full-text products, the issues of compatibility became even more complex. Naturally, more and more people wanted more and more access and variations in computer platforms and equipment became increasingly complex.

Full-text products were created by scanning printed pages. Producers then converted the scanned data into bitmapped images, put them on optical discs and manufactured and distributed the CD-ROMs. Early scanners had fairly high error rates, so a step had to be interposed between scanning and creating the bitmap images, namely, comparing the scan results against the original. All these steps took time, resulting in products that were electronic in character, but appeared some weeks or even months after their paper-based counterparts. Essentially, the CD-ROM products complement traditional paper-based ones, even if end users seem to have a misplaced faith that electronic products are always the most current and complete. What CD-ROMs are best at is solving the problem of mis-placed, misshelved and mutilated journals, as well as "at the bindery" issues. Another, somewhat later, approach was to have libraries load tapes on their local computer system. This basically transferred a number of producer/ publisher problems and costs to the libraries.

Libraries quickly found that this approach took up ever-growing amounts of staff time and created demands for more and more computer memory. Neither CD-ROMs nor local tape loads completely solved the problem of users having remote access to e-resources when the individuals had different computer platforms (PCs and Macs). Most libraries struggled and some still do, with how to provide equal access for each group. "Black boxes" of various types were produced that were supposed to emulate one or the other system—most often to emulate the PC. Very few of these systems really provide complete equality in access and one often heard complaints from Mac users that their needs are ignored. Today the move to Internet/Web-based products has helped to bring a balance to the access issues. Up to a point, any "authorized" user who has access to the Web will have the same access to a product, regardless of the computer platform. The "up to a point" assumes that all users have equivalent computer systems, which is of course not true except perhaps in a special library situation where all employees have the same equipment. In the rest of the world, libraries have a few users with the very latest high-end configurations, many with the current "average" setup and a fairly large number with rather old, slow machines.

Nevertheless, Web-based e-journals and indexing/abstracting services do provide much more equal access for end users. Where the next stage in the migration will come from and take us to is impossible to predict with any degree of assurance. What we do know is that print is still with us and it is likely to be for some time to come.

It is pertinent to note that Hazel Woodward and her colleagues outlined what they called 15 myths about electronic journals. Although they based their article on research they conducted in the United Kingdom (primarily at Loughborough University), we believe the myths they discuss are universal in nature. These myths are:

1. Electronic journals will provide better access to journal articles.
2. Academics and researchers read journals at their office desks.
3. Readers want electronic journals.
4. Electronic journals are quick and convenient to access.
5. Readers know and care who publishes a journal.
6. Readers want page integrity.
7. Electronic journals will bypass libraries and make them redundant.
8. Electronic journals will save libraries money.
9. Storage and dissemination of electronic journals is inexpensive or free.
10. Electronic journals will save paper.
11. Publishers care about readers.
12. Electronic journals will save publishers money.
13. Electronic journals will make subscription agents redundant.
14. Only recent issues of journals are required.
15. All scholarly journals will be available electronically in a few years.

To that extensive list we would add several more "myths":

- Electronic journals are always more current than their print counterparts.
- Electronic journals provide all graphic materials of their print counterparts.
- Electronic journals are always accessible.

- All readers have equal access to required computers at any time.
- Electronic journals will save library staff time and effort in handling serials.

We point out these myths not to suggest that electronic serials are unimportant, but rather to note that they are *not* the final answer to the issues of providing readers with access to the most current and accurate information in the most timely manner. They certainly are important and are the next step in the process, but they are not the ultimate solution as they now exist. Many of the myths exist because the popular press and somewhat overenthusiastic technology people promote the concept beyond its current actual capabilities.

Academic and special librarians have, all too often, encountered a chief financial officer who believes at least one of the myths—that electronic journals will save the library money. We have not found that e-serials save the library money; in fact, they add to the cost of operations, as they are almost always add-ons rather than replacements. Several years ago the senior author's library tried to cover the cost of an aggregator's product, which offered the full text of a large number of journals online, by canceling the paper subscriptions to the titles that would be available electronically. After one year the library reinstated all but five of the paper subscriptions.

A number of reasons caused this to happen. First of all, full text means just that: full text, but not necessarily including graphics. Some products claim to include tables and charts, but in this particular case data was too difficult for users to interpret, so a number of paper subscriptions were quickly restarted. The library had not even thought about ending paper subscriptions for journals that are highly dependent on graphics. (Even in the future, when graphics are consistently available electronically, the library will probably continue the paper subscriptions, as many of the users who want and have remote access to the material do not have computers that can effectively handle graphics). Another reason was the staffs discovery that a surprising number of the electronic titles were a month or more behind the paper versions. That proved unacceptable to several academic departments as well as individual users. Yet another factor was network issues, both on and off campus. Because users were accustomed to finding certain titles on the library's shelves, they still expected the materials to be there when the networks were slow or down. Finally, the volume of printing from the library's public-access printers skyrocketed, even after installation of network printers and charging as much per printed page (without any volume discount) as for the photocopy machines. What the product did accomplish was to give PC and Mac users equal access to the material, as well as providing easier remote access as long the networks were operating properly.

In fact, there are a number of issues to ponder in the interplay between digitized and paper-based serials. One issue is how to provide access. Digital serials, in theory, are accessible any-where, anytime, as long as there is a connection between a computer and the database containing the desired material. Many customers and technology supporters see this as the ideal future anywhere at any time.

Library literature generally approaches this issue in terms of ownership versus access. When a library subscribes to a paper journal, the library owns the copies of those titles, for which it paid the appropriate fee. Electronic formats are often a different matter. Producers of electronic material usually include a license agreement that limits the library's ability to use the material and normally states that the library has access rights only so long as the annual fee is current. In essence, the library only leases the data.

If a library has any responsibility for long-term retention of information, leasing is a problematic policy even if the producer says it will archive the files and gives the library the right to access the files for the years for which it paid a lease fee. Other aspects of serials are the issues of "just-in-case" and "just-in time." Long-term preservation is, in a sense, "just-in-case". That is, someone at some time will require the information. "Just-in-time" is locating the de-material at the time the user needs it, most often from somewhere other than the home library collection. Digitized data makes just-in-time delivery a realistic option. One reality is that fewer and fewer libraries can continue to subscribe to thousands of serial titles just-in-case. If there is a paper subscription, it must be for high-demand items, not the seldom-used titles.

Leasing and just-in-time delivery work well, but one cannot help but wonder (as we did in chapter 6), about how far profit-oriented producers will go to maintain backfiles, or, for that matter, who will still be in business 20 years in the future. There are serious concerns about who, how and for how long electronic data will be available (archived).

No a doubt, digitized serials are a mixed blessing. They are very popular, they provide more flexibility in searching than their paper-based counterparts and remote access at any time is a possibility. Although they do not reduce library operating costs, they do present new challenges for public service staff. Electronic systems can fail, as do power supplies, causing customer and staff frustration. Also, as anyone who has spent much time with Internet-based services knows, "electronic" does not always translate into "fast".

On the one hand, waiting for files to download, waiting to have a server "accept" your query, or being abruptly cut off in mid-session are sources of frustration that do not exist with paper-based serials. On the other hand, torn-out articles, misshelved or missing volumes, or holiday library closures are not problems with the electronic serials (provided offset access to the required systems is available).

Without question, e-serials will be increasingly important in any overall collection development plan for any type of library. Thus, one must understand their benefits as well as their demerits.

How to Select E-Serials?

Is the process of selecting e-serials different from that followed for print serials? The answer is no, not really; however, there are some additional steps. We believe that all the factors that apply to selecting paper titles also apply to e-journals. One factor that differs is that often, at least in the case of journal aggregator services, the purchasing decision is made for a package of titles rather than title by title. That in turn means that the cost being considered is substantially higher than for any single typical library paper subscription. Thus, one adds factors of new costs, vendor support and a "package" of titles. Another factor complicating the decision is that electronic resource decisions involve more staff than is typical for paper-based selection decisions. If nothing else, there are questions about technology requirements and capabilities that systems staff must answer.

In addition, more of the public service staff are involved in supporting users of electronic resources. Few users need assistance in opening a paper journal, but many may need it when locating and using an electronic title. Packages from either producers or other vendors often employ different search engines; this requires staff to remember which database operates in which manner. Thus, public service staff often want a voice in deciding what, if any, new electronic products to add to the service program.

Remarkably, Mary Jean Pavelsek outlined a set of 11 "guidelines" for evaluating journals and their providers.

1. Economics
2. Ease of use/User flexibility
3. Archival implications
4. Future accessibility
5. Access
6. Licensing, copyright and distribution restrictions
7. Single or multiple publisher
8. Print vs. electronic comparisons
9. User support
10. If a package, is it "all or nothing"?
11. Planned enhancements.

To her list we would add cost per user, technological issues and aggregators. We have mentioned the two typical methods for securing e-serials: direct from the publishers/producers or from so-called aggregators.

An *aggregator* is an organization that develops "packages" of electronic serials. The aggregator enters into contracts with a number of publishers/producers to offer their titles as a group. Producers gain by not having to invest as much in marketing, programming and technology. Then the aggregator adds value to the package by providing a consistent search engine for searching all the titles.

Naturally, aggregators then add a charge for their services on top of what the cost was from the producers, often in the 30 to 40 percent range. Some of the large aggregators are OCLC, Bell & Howell Information and Learning Company, Lexis/Nexis and EBSCO. Deciding on aggregator packages usually entails accepting a number—sometimes a substantial number—of titles one would never subscribe to in print. Few of the aggregators allow a library to take only the titles of interest. Naturally, that means the library pays for titles it does not want. Thus, one question to consider is if the overall cost is really appropriate for the number of titles the library *does* want. One interesting effort in 1999 was the California State University System's issuance of a Request for Proposal (RFP) to aggregators to supply access to a list of 1,279 journals on what the System calls the "Journal Access Core Collection". The titles on the list are those in highest demand in the System's 23 libraries. At the time we prepared this edition. There was no indication of how successful the RFP would be in providing access to just the titles desired rather than titles to which the aggregators have easy access.

Content concerns relate to the usual subject issues and also to how complete the material is, assuming there is a print counterpart. Another concern should be whether there are "additions" to the product and whether they are necessary or beneficial. Some vendors/producers add some form of multimedia—sound or video clips—to their material. Often this is of the "gee whiz, look what technology allows us to do" variety rather than being a true added value.

Such additions create hardware and software compatibility problems for some library-owned and certainly for some remote users' machines. Another issue to consider is what the library can or cannot do with the electronic material. Some vendors place restrictions on who can use the material, even in a public access setting.

Such restrictions create problems for the public service staff—how to identify user types and monitoring what is being used. For example, *Academic* Universe from Lexis/Nexis is contractually limited to the students, staff and faculty of the purchasing institution. Individuals not affiliated with the institution are not permitted to use the service. What happens if the purchase was through a consortium and a person is visiting another campus that is part of the consortium? Can the visitor use the service without violating the license agreement, since the home institution also has the service? Logically, one would think that such use would be acceptable; however, unless the consortium's agreement so indicates, there is a chance that such use would be a violation. Another concern is that all contracts call for the purchaser to be responsible for copyright violations. The whole question of license agreements is complex.

Finally, long-term access to and preservation of material is usually a concern. Who will archive the material? How will it be archived and for how long? These are questions one needs to consider at the point of making a selection decision. Programs operated by libraries, such as JSTOR, are more likely to provide the electronic long-term archiving that both librarians. And scholars expect with print materials. Commercial ventures are profit-driven and are unlikely to maintain a service that loses money for very long.

Handling E-Serials

Unlike a print subscription, after the appropriate

recordkeeping files are in place, e-serials require more setup steps. Generally a new print subscription merely goes into its appropriate place with the other current issues of the print journals. In the case of e-serials, as we mentioned in the section on selection, someone must assure that the technical issues have been addressed before the service is implemented. If the access is Web-based and domain in nature, providing IP ranges is fairly straightforward. However, password verification is still a requirement of some systems and libraries must decide who will have access to these passwords.

Will patrons be logged on individually, or will certain patrons (such as faculty members) be given the password to use as needed? There must be testing to determine compatibility with other services (changes in hardware or software configurations, for example). Libraries must also consider what, if anything, will appear in the library's OPAC about the product. If a package of, say, 1,000 full-text journals is purchased, will the library add a note to the holdings statements for titles the library also has in a print format? What about entries for the "new" titles, even those that may not be important to the library's customer base? Will the OPAC reflect just title, electronic address only, or both? Will there be a "hot link" in the OPAC or on the library Website? If images are included in the package, does the library need "helper" applications installed on its public machines?

Every library using electronic materials needs one person or office that handles and maintains a file of license agreements. Someone must review the agreement and notify staff of any new requirements. Public service staff will need time for familiarization and training in using the new product. Vendor support telephone numbers and/or Internet addresses should be available to staff. End users may also need assistance, especially if they want to print, e-mail, or download an article from the product for the first or second time. If the journals are accessible from offsite, whether through a proxy server or other means, what support exists in the library and at the institution for offsite patrons who have trouble using the resource?

A good article outlining all the steps and issues in implementing a new e-serial is Cindy Stewart Kang's "Collection Development for Online Serials".6 In 1998, Janet Hughes and Catherine Lee published an interesting article that can serve as a case study of the process of selecting, acquiring and implementing a full-text journal package. Part of what makes this article interesting is that it addresses issues related to multiple service points. The authors described the process used at Pennsylvania State University and its statewide 23-campus system. They concluded by stating, "Overall, although the experience of implementing the first networked full-text databases at Penn State was a positive one, its success depended upon careful planning and dedicated interdepartmental and campus cooperation. These qualities will be needed to make future forays into full-text equally successful".

Scholarly journals, magazines, newspapers and the like. There is a type of literature that does not receive much discussion, the so-called grey literature. In the past, some research and special libraries made an effort to collect this type of material. Today, with electronic "publishing" on the Internet a fact of life, grey literature takes on a new meaning. Grey literature was and is primarily of scholarly interest, particularly in the sciences and tends to be the output of the "invisible college". A widely accepted definition of grey literature has yet to be formulated.

Harrod's Librarians' Glossary defines these items as "semipublished material, for example reports, internal documents, theses, etc. not formally published or available commercially and consequently difficult to trace bibliographically". Julia Gelfand stated, "The definition of grey literature has changed rather drastically since the First International Conference, held in Amsterdam, four years ago [1993]".

One of the reasons for the changing nature of the concept of grey literature is electronic publishing. To some degree, what we now call the Internet was developed so that scientists and scholars could more quickly share results (grey literature) and work together from different physical locations (the invisible college).

Today, technology and the Internet are creating new types of grey literature, not just online preprint services and technical report access. Perhaps the most striking change is the ability to describe phenomena in other than textual terms—modelling online, movement, sound and true interactive collaborative work. Julia Gelfand suggested, Learning about this new grey literature is in itself a non-traditional role for librarians and scholars .... Training and bibliographic familiarity in this age is indeed quite different, because one does not follow a curriculum or set of readers or textbooks, but instead studies by doing, engaging in online time, discovering what the digital literati in different fields contribute as resources for good, appropriate, critical, sought after information. Usually, a strong needs assessment for the information, coupled with this new facility in making it readily available without enhanced packaging, encourages its use.

Now a question arises—Is grey literature a serial? As it tends to be ongoing in nature, one can consider it at least a semi-serial. To what degree the library tries to provide access to such material is very much a matter of local need and close collaboration between the library and its users.

Document Delivery

In the past, traditional interlibrary loan (ILL) services often provided the only access to materials not owned, especially to grey literature. Today libraries have a choice in how to provide customers with needed but unowned materials. There are at least seven broad types of document delivery services in addition to the traditional ILL: general commercial services, specialized commercial services, direct from publisher/producer, aggregator services, national library collections, information brokers and fee-based services in a large research library.

Why are libraries turning to this approach and how does it relate to collection development? The answer to the relationship question resides in how a given library decides to address the issues of access or ownership. The more material a library knows it must own, the greater the work for the collection development officers. Even when employing document delivery to provide "just in time" access to very low-use materials, there is a need for collection development staff to coordinate their activities with those of document delivery.

Essentially, there must be ongoing planning and coordination of both activities. The answer to why use services other than traditional ILL is more complex. Certainly a major factor is the escalating costs of serials, which far outpace inflation in other areas of the economy and library budgets that are hard-pressed to do more than maintain constant collection levels, much less increase their size. Almost every library of any size has had to implement at least one journal reduction exercise some time in the last 15 years. Many libraries have had to undertake several such cutting efforts in the recent past.

The first such program is relatively easy, as there are usually a number of titles that were acquired for the "just-in-case" need and show little or no use over time. Depending upon the size of the necessary reduction, perhaps the first time will only have to "hit" very low-use titles; in those cases, depending on ILL to fulfill the rare request may be an adequate alternative.

Unfortunately, most of the reductions in serials collections have cut more deeply, which required thinking about how to supply the wanted material more quickly than traditional ILL. Also an issue is how much of an increase in ILL requests the existing staff can handle. If there are alternatives that allow the requestor to have direct access to the document-supplying service, there will be little or no increase in the ILL workload. Another factor, at least for a few libraries, relates to space and money. Libraries have had difficulty maintaining their operating budgets; when it comes to securing funding for additional space to house the ever-growing collections, the track record is even bleaker.

One way to gain space in an existing facility is to look at long back runs of journals, especially those that have very little usage. Withdrawing the physical volumes will provide shelving space. The question then becomes how to provide access to the withdrawn titles. Certainly, buying microfiche/film versions is one option; however, microfilm storage cabinets take up space and the cost of the microforms and the equipment to use them must be considered.

Going with a document delivery option saves space and the cost of requested materials may never equal the cost of the microforms. Gale Etschmaier and Marifran Bustion discussed the pro and cons of such services in an article about the experience of Gelman Library at George Washington University in implementing a document delivery service. The situation they described was a major journal cancellation project in which the library cancelled 1,031 journal titles in 1993-1994. One of their interesting findings was that, as of early 1997, only 35 of those titles (roughly 3 percent) had been the subject of any requests for articles. They concluded by stating, "The data gathered through monitoring direct requests through document delivery and interlibrary loan services can be monitored and analyzed as an aid to collection development".

When evaluating possible document delivery services, one should use most of the factors one employs to assess any vendor. The additional elements to consider are similar to those for choosing an e-journal vendor:

1) Type of access provided
2) Quality/content of the database
3) Ordering options (user, library)
4) Costs and what is covered (copyright fees)
5) Delivery options (fax, e-mail, overnight mail)
6) Reliability (does the service meet advertised delivery times?)
7) Payment options (credit card, invoices, prepaid deposit)
8) Customer service availability (end users, staff only)

Pricing

In fact, e-serials do not save either the producer or the library money. Perhaps at some point in the past there was a reasonable expectation of such savings. However, by the mid-1990s it was clear to both vendors and libraries that this would not be the case. For example, as Robert Marks noted, the American Chemical Society estimated that its CD-ROM journals cost 25 to 33 percent more to produce than their print versions. The higher cost was attributed to the need to provide and maintain a search engine. In another article, Tom Abate reported the American Institute of Physics' estimate that providing both a print and electronic copy of a title cost between 10 and 15 percent more than just offering a print version of the same title.

Conversations with publishers of electronic-only serials indicate that they see no difference in costs; they claim it costs just as much for an e-only version as it does for print-only. Janet Fischer of MIT Press medicated that the reason producers of e-only serials see costs as equal was not so much a function of production costs as it was an overall loss of revenue— no back-issue sales, no renting of subscriber mailing lists and, perhaps most importantly, the loss of advertising income. The dual pricing one found and still finds with many scholarly print serials (that is, one price for individuals and a higher price for institutions) continues in the electronic environment, if in a slightly different guise. Individuals do not face the same licensing issues as libraries and do not pay for more than one user, nor are they asked about number of potential users in the household or office. Libraries usually have to pay extra fees, rather substantial at times, for more than one simultaneous user license.

Different producers use different increments, such as 1 to 4 users at one rate, 5 to 9 another rate and so on to a rate for unlimited access. Another pricing mechanism is by size of the service population, frequently based upon the number of full-time students or staff (full-time equivalent or FTE) at an institution. This is probably one of the most costly approaches for libraries when it comes to specialized serials and products.

Transaction-based fees are another pricing mechanism that can drive up the cost of electronic serials for a library (this is the model that OCLC was using for First Search in the late 1990s). In some ways, this approach is less costly than the FTE model, as actual usage determines the price. One drawback of this model is that the library is never certain what its costs will be until after the fact. With First Search, OCLC (at least with consortiums) sets an annual fee that includes a fixed number of searches. The fee is paid in advance and at the end of the year there may be additional charges if the search limit was exceeded. The amount may be something of a shock for the library, if it has not been carefully monitoring usage. (The Loyola Marymount University library belongs to a consortium that purchased access to First Search and members discussed what databases they could "turn oft" to control the year-end charges. Somehow it seems strange to buy access to a database and then have to discuss which ones we should restrict public access to in order to save money). Part of the problem with the transaction-based approach is that every search *counts,* even those in which the searcher has misspelled a word or does not understand how to search the database. It is difficult to know how much value for money expended one actually receives from this model. At least with paper formats user and staff mistakes do not cost the library additional money. When buying a package from an aggregator, the library knows it will be paying an extra fee for the "added value" of having a single source and search engine for journals from a variety of producers.

However, one often is buying access to titles of little or no interest to the library's service population, because a package truly is all or nothing. This effectively drives up the cost of the titles that are of interest to the library users. Some publishers/producers, at least in 1999, have not decided which model to follow. As a result, some offer free access to an electronic version of a title if the library has a subscription to the print format. Others offer such access for a modest fee (10 to 15 percent) above the print subscription cost. Where the pricing will go is difficult to predict beyond the fact that prices will continue to escalate.

As Bill Robnett stated, "The complexities of online serials pricing may increase as more publishers enter the electronic publishing market. ... One consideration is that serials budgets will be redefined as libraries purchase access in units of articles, an open-ended concept quite different from the now prevalent subcription".

To sum up, it can be surmised that Electronic serials are probably the "wave of the future", but perhaps a more distant future than technology enthusiasts would have us believe. Despite the advantages of having materials available in such formats, it appears that there is little prospect of either producers or libraries realizing any cost savings as a result of migrating to an electronic environment. How libraries will handle the ever-escalating costs of serials, regardless of format, is something to be given a serious thought.

REFERENCES

Abate, Tom. "Publishing Scientific Journals Online". *Bioscience* 47 (March 1997): 175-79.

American Library Association. 'Directory of Union Lists of Serials". *Serials Review* 14, nos. 1/2 (1998): 115-59.

Barnes, J. H. "One Giant Leap, One Small Step: Continuing the Migration to Electronic Journals". *Library Trends* 45 (Winter 1997): 404-15.

Cameron R. D. 'Not Just E-Journals: Providing and Maintaining Access to Serials and Serials Information Through the World-Wide Web". *Serials Librarian* 29, nos. 3/4 (1996): 209-22.

Cline, N. M. "Local or Remote Access: Choices and Issues". *Collection Management* 22, nos. 3-4 (1998): 21-29.

Cole, J. E. and J. W. Williams, eds. *Serials Management in the Electronic Era.* New York: Haworth Press, 1996.

Davis, T. "Evolution of Selection Activities for Electronic Resources". *Library Trends* 45 (Winter 1997): 391-403.

Donnice, C. and E. F. Jurries. "An Idea Whose Time Has Come: The Alliance Electronic Journal Access·Web Site", *Colorado Libraries* 22 (Summer 1996): 15-19.

Duranceau, E. F. "Beyond Print: Revisioning Serials Acquisitions for the Digital Age". *Serials Librarian* 33, nos. 1-2 (1998): 83-105.

Fritseh, D. "A Capital Idea: Electronic Serials from Acquisition to Access". *Serials Review* 23 (Winter 1997): 83-88.

Gadd, E. "Copyright Clearance for the Digital Library". *Serials* 10 (March 1997): 27-32.

Gilbert, N. "Aggregators of Electronic Journals". 1997. Available via e-mail from <LIBLICENSE-L@PANTHE-ON.YALE.EDU>.

"Gordon, B. and M. A. Sheble. 'Archiving Electronic Journals". *Serials Review* 21 (Winter 1995): 13-21.

Guernsey, L. "Library Groups, Decrying 'Excessive Pricing,' Demand New Policies on Electronic Journals". *Chronicle of Higher Education* 44, no. 31 (1998): A33-34.

Guthrie, K. M. and W. P. Lougee. 'The JSTOR Solution: Accessing and Preserving the Past". *Library Journal* 122, no. 2 (1998): 42-44.

Harter, S. P. and H. K. Kin. "Accessing Electronic Journals and Other Publications". *College & Research Libraries* 57 (September 1996): 440-56.

Hawbaker, A. C. and C. K.Wagner. "Periodical Ownership Versus Fulltext Online Access: A Cost-Benefit Analysis". *Journal of Academic Librarianship* 22, no. 2 (1996): 105-9.

Hawkins, L. "Network Accessed Scholarly Serials". *Serials Librarian* 29, nos. 3/4 (1996): 19-31.

Homan, J. M. "Precocious Dinosaur or Preeminent Electronic Resource?" *Bulletin of the Medical Library Association* 85 (January 1997): 59-60.

Hruska, M. "Remote Internet Serials in the OPAC?" *Serials Review* 21 (Winter 1995): 68-70.

Ingoldsby, T. C. "Electronic Publishing from the Producers' Point-of-View". In *National Online Meeting Proceedings—18th*. New York: Information Today, 1997.

Jeapes, B. 'Learning to Live with E-Journals". *Electronic Library* 15 (February 1997): 27-30.

Ketcham, L. and K Born. "Projecting Electronic Revolution While Budgeting for the Status Quo". *Library Journal* 121 (April 15, 1996): 45-53.

Ketcham-Van Orsdel, *L. a*nd K. Born. "E-Journals Come of Age". *Library Journal* 123 (April 15, 1998): 40-45.

Knight, N. H. "Electronic Pubs Pricing in the Web Era". *Information Today* 15 (September 1998): 39-40.

Machovec, G. S. "Electronic Journal Market Overview—1997". *Serials Review* 23 (Summer 1997): 31-44.

McKay, S. C. "Partnering in a Changing Medium". *Library Acquisition: Practice and Theory* 22, no. 1 (1998): 23-27.

McMillan, G. "Technical Processing of Electronic Journals". *Library Resources & Technical Services* 36 (October 1992): 470-72.

Metz, P., et al. "A Standardized Form for Evaluation and Description of Electronic Resources Under Consideration by the Virginia Tech University Libraries". *Technicalities* 18, no. 10 (November/December 1998): 9-10.

Miller, W. "Electronic Access to Information Will Not Reduce the Cost of Library Materials". *Library Issues: Briefings for Faculty and Administrators* 15, no. 6 (July 1995): 1-4.

Moothart, T. "Providing Access to E-Journals Through Library Home Pages". *Serials Review* 22 (Summer 1996): 71-77.

Pikowsky, R.A. "Electronic Journals as a Potential Solution to Escalating Serials Cost". *Serials Librarian* 32, nos. 3/4 (1997): 31-56.

Rowland, J. F. "Electronic Journals: Delivery, Use and Access". *IFLA Journal* 22, no. 3 (1996): 226-28.

Simser, C. N. and M. A. Somers, eds. *Experimentation and Collaboration: Creating Serials for a New Millennium.* New York: Haworth Press, 1998.

7

Role of Intergovernmental Organisations

> "We are made for cooperation, like feet like hands, like eyelids, like the rows of the upper and lower teeth. To act against one another then is contrary to Nature, and it is acting against one another to be vexed and turn away."
>
> —***Marcus Aurelius***

Universal access to information has become a priority programme for the peoples of the world. Currently, however, the flow of information tends substantially to be between the educationally elite or to be one way—from West to East or from the developed countries to the underdeveloped.

Due to the development of modern communications, all the countries of the world have become relatively near neighbours and the exploration of space is proceeding purposively. Against this background it is very difficult for any country to remain isolated in its traditional way of life. Television, the radio, the eradication of illiteracy, and the development of higher education have generated an unprecedented demand for information.

It is remarkable that the need to facilitate the worldwide flow of information in order to offer universal access to information is becoming increasingly important. Libraries and information services have an important role to play in encouraging universal access to information. They have so far understandably given priority, to Universal Bibliographical Control (UBC) and Universal Availability of Publications (UAP). This is, however, a start only. The next stage is the encouragement of Universal Access to Information (UAI), a programme which this book hopes to foster. The development of computer-based services in recent years suggests that UAI is achievable.

Notably a step towards UAI was the project on the International Flow of Information sponsored in 1979 by the US International Communication Agency, the Library of Congress, and the Graduate School of Library Studies, University of Hawaii. This was followed by a tour of libraries and information services in the USA by a group of international information and library specialists. The participants were made well aware of the consequences of the development of computer-based services in making progress possible towards universal access to information, but concern was expressed that this should not be one way. The flow of information should be from East to West as well as from West to East. It should be from the developing countries to the developed countries as well as from the developed countries to the developing. This is in tune with the Third World's desire for a New World Information Order, which we have referred to as UAI.

Certainly the lack of effective international communication has been one reason for the current difficulties in the Middle East, and it has long been a major barrier between Communist countries with their aspirations to thought control and countries which believe in freedom of access to information of all kinds. Intergovernmental organisations have a key part to play in encouraging the free flow of information between the various countries of the world. Their recent activities have been large scale and world wide, involving the production of large numbers of documents of many kinds, and the sponsorship of many conferences and visits of experts at the political and the professional level.

The sheer size of the information explosion, linguistic barriers, and educational limitations are a few of the factors which have prevented greater progress in the free flow of information.

There have, however, been two developments which illustrate the efforts of Intergovernmental organisations to encourage the flow of information: (i) the efforts of UNO to improve its own documentation and information services; and (ii) its encouragement and support of UNESCO to foster the development worldwide of information policies through (World Science Information System (UNISIST) (National Information Systems), and (NATIS) (General Information Programme (GIP). These are steps towards the achievement of UAI.

In fact, UNO's difficulties in providing effective documentation and information services about its own activities arise from the very wide scale of its library and information responsibilities. UNO maintains a headquarters library in New York and a library at Geneva. The principal purpose of these libraries is to assist the General Assembly, the Security Council, and the Trusteeship Council of the United Nations to discharge their responsibilities. UNO libraries need, however, to discharge a special function as leaders in international librarianship by encouraging international co-operation and standardisation in all fields of librarianship, documentation, and information services.

UNO should reach out to assist all agencies which can contribute to the basic international function of UNO—to help maintain international peace and security, to develop friendly relations between nations, and international co-operation in solving international, social, cultural, and humanitarian problems through its Economic and Social Council (ECOSOC).

This aims at promoting higher standards of living and economic and social development through the important UNO agencies which it supervises—the Technical Assistance Board (TAB), the Drug Supervisory Board (DSB), the United Nations Children's Emergency Fund (UNICEF), and the United Nations Commissions for Refugees (UNHCR), and through such regional and functional commissions as the Economic Commission for Europe (ECE), the Economic Commission for Latin America (ECLA), etc.

Remarkably, a number of agencies (with relationships with UNO defined by individual agreements) provide specialised library and information services—the International Monetary Fund (IMF), the International Bank for Reconstruction and Development (IBRD), commonly known as the World Bank, the International Civil Aviation Organisation, the World Meteorological Organisation, the World Health Organisation, and UNESCO.

The large number of documents produced by international agencies and the lack of standardization had by 1970 produced a crisis. By 1970 UNO was producing nearly one billion units of documentation annually. The problem of organising these documents to facilitate quick and convenient access was proving to be very difficult.

Lester Pearson put the problem succinctly: "The United Nations is drowning in its own words and suffocating in its own documentation. Over communication was tending to conceal pertinent information necessary for decision making. Increasingly, UNO was being impelled to adopt more effective policies to secure bibliographical control of these documents and improved access to them. A Joint Inspection Unit was therefore appointed to consider the problem of documentation and the need to formulate information policies. This recognition by UNO of its own need for information policies was one of the many factors which led UNESCO to encourage the worldwide formulation of information policies through sponsorship successively of UNISIST, NATIS, and GIP.

The Joint Inspection Unit of UNO reported in 1971—the year when UNISIST was launched—that the future usefulness of UNO might depend on its ability to control and exploit its own documentation. In the early 1970s over a million UNO documents were unindexed and the number was increasing by over 100,000 per annum. It had clearly become essential for UNO to develop its own information policy. The United Nations Documents Index (UNDEX) did not cover more than 10% of the documents then issued. In view of UNO's failure to control and effectively exploit the information which it was producing, grater efforts were made to reduce the number of documents produced, to define policies, to reduce the burden of unnecessary documentation, and to develop computerisation of indexes.

In 1972 an International Symposium of the Documentation of the United Nations and other Intergovernmental Organisations was held in Geneva, but the continued failure to make rapid progress is illustrated by the fact that the proceedings of the Symposium were not published until 1974 under the title Utilisation of International Documentation. Some of the statements made at the Symposium indicated the directions in which progress was to be made: "international" organisations have not so far adopted any consistent information policy, thus ruling out any possibility of establishing and operating an information systems"; "one means of improving a country's control over intergovernmental publications is to formulate a national acquisitions policy"; "sound information policy should recognise that the increase in international data and the growing interdependence between nations and between the various fields of international activity will add to-rather than diminish—the quantity of information needed".

It was further recommended, with a high priority to Governments that were members of the various organisations—both within and outside the United Nations system—to formulate and support a suitable information policy and to apply it in a consistent way. Few Governments have been successful in this connection, but some worldwide progress has been made. For its part UNO has also only achieved limited success, mainly through its computerisation programme. It was left to UNESCO to encourage the development of information policies in countries throughout the world, while UNO continued its efforts to try to set an example. It organised a Second World Symposium on International Documentation in 1980 in Brussels at which emphasis was not on policies but upon "complex aspects and problems of international information and documentation".

UNESCO

UNESCO has devoted much attention during the last decade to the encouragement of the development of international and national information policies and systems, commencing in 1971 with the concept of UNISIST, which was reinforced in 1974 by the concept of NATIS and extended in 1977 to the concept of GIP. A common thread throughout all three concepts is the need to develop international and national library and information policies and to plan for their systematic implementation.

Whilst these concepts have encouraged some considerable developments in international and national library and information services and programmes, they have been the subject of much criticism and dissatisfaction because the results have bees so disappointing. Some of this disappointment was due to lack of appreciation of the difficulties of providing unpublished information. Under the terms of the agreement between UNO and UNESCO in 1946, UNESCO was "to initiate methods of international co-operation to give the people of all countries access to the printed and published materials produced by any of them". Unpublished information, much of which is confidential, was excluded. But the UNISIST programme raised disappointed expectations that the know-how of the developed countries could be made easily available to the developing countries.

World Science Information System (UNISIST)

The Intergovernmental Conference to advise the Director General of UNESCO on UNISIST met in Paris in 1971, but the developed countries indicated that no additional money would be provided by them for the purposes of UNISIST. This would have to be funded by UNESCO out of its normal budget and in accordance with UNESCO's priorities. Hence progress was inevitably slow. It was not until 1973 that the first UNISIST Newsletter appeared. This set out the priority objectives of UNISIST—improving systems interconnection, strengthening the role of the institutional components of the information transfer chain, developing specialised information manpower, development of scientific information policies, and giving assistance to developing countries in the creation of scientific and technical information infrastructures. In July 1973 the Director General of UNESCO addressed a circular letter to member States inviting Governments to establish UNISIST National Committees and to designate a Governmental agency to act as a national focal point for the UNISIST programme. The circular indicated that the essential functions of a national focal point were to be concerned with policy. The focal point was to serve as a co-ordinating mechanism rather than as a operational body. Its policy functions were to be general and would cover all disciplines.

There would normally be satellite focal points for special interests. The purpose of the focal point was to ensure that the total efforts, however dispersed, was on the right scale, properly balanced and making the best use of available resources. The main functions were to develop primary communications, to review information needs, to develop scientific libraries and arrange for translations, to ensure the provision of indexing and abstracting services, to foster information analysis and data compilation centers, to fill gaps in national information services, to foster information transfer networks, to promote study of pricing policy and legal and administrative problems, to adopt international standards of bibliographical description, etc., to foster research and training, to support information research and development, to encourage specialised focal points, to promote aid to developing countries, and to ensure that a good case was made for financial resources.

In fact focal points were, in discharge of their responsibilities, to stimulate, support, and co-ordinate research, co-operate with focal points in other countries and regional and international focal points. The focal point was ideally to be located in the office of the Chief Minister or of the Cabinet, or in a department concerned with science or with the media or an interdepartmental committee. Members of the committee of the focal point were, as far as possible, to have information responsibilities in their departments. The chairman should be able to knit together the thinking of departments with strongly entrenched interests, perhaps even with a predisposition to avoid co-operation altogether, and should in all probability be drawn from the department or agency in which the focal point was placed.

The relationship between the inter-departmental committee and the national committee for UNISIST needed to be defined with care. The focal point would normally provide the secretariat for the UNISIST national committee. A number of countries had, of course, already established focal points for scientific and technical information, before the advent of UNISIST, and these became also focal points for its programme. For example, the US National Science Foundation's Office of Scientific Information Service had by Executive Order 10,807 of 17 March, 1979 been given responsibility for providing "leadership in the effective co-ordination of the scientific information activities of the Federal Government".

Well over a decade latter, the President of the Franklin Institute (Bowen C. Dees) issued a statement—on 12 June 1975—in which he indicated that it was not "easy to determine how to provide the maximum flow of science and technology information...to all those in the United States who should be provided such information...The attempts made thus far to find mechanisms for dealing separately with the federal and non-federal elements of this problem area have not achieved notable success".

Few would argue against the proposition that primary responsibility lies with the Federal Government:

(i) for formulating national science and technology information policies that can strengthen development and application of the country's scientific and technological resources;

(ii) for managing and co-ordinating the Federal Government's own information activities in the fields; and

(iii) for fully employing the capabilities of the private sector in disseminating and promoting and the use of science and technology information.

Bowen C. Dees understood the difficulties of a focal point more fully than the authors of the UNISIST statement on focal points. He wrote that a focal point "had reason to fear undertaking a task which would necessitate confrontations with much larger and more fully established agencies". He stressed "the difficulties that must always be faced when one agency provides or attempts to provide leadership in co-ordinating the programmes of many other agencies". Such a leadership cannot be based on authority but must be centred in aiming at completely voluntary co-operation. This co-operation will be more easily forthcoming if it is shown to be in the direct interest of the co-operating organisations. Decisions as to the allocation of finances and other resources to library and information services must be determined at a higher level than that of the scientist or information scientist—at the level of the head of the Government department or other agency responsible for giving priority to activities necessary to implement the major programmes assigned to it. Details will be given in the chapters on the services in various continents of the difficulties of national focal points in obtaining resources to discharge their responsibilities unless they are able to identify activities which attract voluntary self-interested co-operation. In spite of all the difficulties, a considerable number of countries established national focal points for UNISIST following the invitation from the Director General of UNESCO for them to do so.

Few of them achieved more than a very modest success. The developments which could be firmly ascribed to the establishment of focal points were few and they tended, in some cases, to be related not to scientific and technical information *per se* but to bibliographical activities such as the programme for UBC and the associated library programme ISBNs (International Standard Book Numbers). These were properly the province of other international organisations such as the International Federation of Library Associations and Institutions (IFLA).

Nevertheless, the concept of UNISIST was very important and it did encourage the need to devote more resources for library and information services. Through funds provided by the United Nations Development Programme (UNDP) international meetings were arranged by UNESCO to bring together representatives from many countries to consider scientific and technical information questions in connection with the UNISIST programme. Experimental national programme were financed in a number of developing countries—Colombia, Indonesia, Korea, etc., with mixed success. Although the end products of these activities were rarely completely satisfactory, opportunities were given to potential information specialists to meet together and to get to know each other.

National Information Systems (NATIS)

Dissatisfaction with the performance of the UNISIST

programme was in all probability one of the reasons why UNESCO decided to sponsor the new international concept of NATIS. Certainly it had become clearer that an information system linked to science and technology alone was unsatisfactory. Indeed, UNISIST had decided to extend its programme to the social science before the decision of UNESCO to sponsor NATIS.

Increasingly, however, it was being recognized that science and technology were not only linked closely to the social sciences, because of their impact on society, but also to the humanities, because of their impact on the quality of life. Nevertheless, UNISIST continued to operate its specialist programme, organizing, for example, meetings in the Federal Republic of Germany in 1978, in Poland in 1979, and in the USA in 1980.

Further the International Conference on the Planning of National Documentation, Libraries, and Archives Infrastructures was organised in Paris in 1974 in co-operation with the International Federation for Documentation (FID), IFLA, and the International Council on Archives (ICA). Its resolutions supported the foundation of NATIS for all subjects and all categories of users.

UNISCO urged Member States to:

(i) Review at the highest level existing arrangements, both national and international, for providing access to information.

(ii) Draw up plans for improving the existing arrangements.

The recommendations of the Intergovernmental Conference were approved by the General Conference of UNESCO. The Director General of UNESCO was authrorised to draw up a long-term programme for the implementation of NATIS to be considered at the 19th session of UNESCO in 1976, and to issue not later than December 1976 general guidelines for the implementation of NATIS. The guidelines covered *National Information Policy* (UNESCO, Paris, 1976), *Design and Planning of National Information Systems* (UNESCO, Paris, 1976), and Establishing a *Legislative Framework for the Implementation of NATIS* (UNESCO, Paris, 1976).

The paper *National Information Policy* started by defining the term library to cover not only libraries in the traditional sense but also documentation centers and information centres: "A Library is a collection of records whether published or unpublished. The records are usually but not necessarily documents."

This definition followed the general principles expressed over a decade earlier in *Modern Documentation and Information Practices*, published by FID with the assistance of UNESCO under the general editorship of Dr. O. Frank: "Apart from libraries in the classical sense of the word, there are special libraries, information centers or services and departments...documentary and bibliographical centers...Arguments about which names should be assigned to these various functions...are largely verbal and vary according to circumstances and nationality."

In *Libraries in the Modern World* (G. Chandler, 1965) this concept is taken one stage further. It is proposed that librarians, special librarians, documentation officers (including archivists), and information officers are all concerned primarily with the organization and making available of information in the broadest sense of the term. The distinction between the librarian, the special librarian, the documentation officer, the archivist, and the information officer did not rest upon fundamental professional differences but on the degree of subject specialization required in the handling of books, documents, and information data which formed part of the collections controlled. But the general term, library, was an appropriate term to describe the common functions with the addition of such qualifying words as were necessary, e.g., Library of the Performing Arts. If this definition had been accepted the conflict between UNISISTS, NATIS, AND GIP might have been avoided, IFLA, FID, and ICA might have joined together to form a more effective organization. This might have obtained more support both nationally and internationally.

National libraries which have made the most progress recently are precisely those which combine specialist library, documentation, and information functions, e.g. the Bibliotheque Royale, Belgium, the Library of Congress, the British Library, and the National Library of Australia, etc. The paper *National Information Policy* accepted that: "all Government departments need an adequate information system, and some, such as those concerned with economic planning, trade and industry, agriculture, social welfare and education, have a special interest in the supply of information." It is difficult however, to accept the statement in *National Information Policy* that: "to leave each department interested to decide its own information policy, as is often the case at present, produces an un-co-ordinated bunch of arrangements". This show an inadequate appreciation of the fact that Governments determine social priorities at the highest level and often have scientific and other advisory groups to advise them on policy.

When priorities have been determined by Governments, they are referred to the appropriate departments or groups of departments to implement. The responsibility to implement appropriate approved policy priorities rests with the departmental head. It is his responsibility, therefore, to determine the level of library and information services to which priority is to be given.

In many countries Governmental librarians have established formal and informal means of co-operation without finding it necessary to appoint a co-ordinator to impose co-operation. Hence the NATIS committees, when established, ought to have concentrated on positive ways of resource-sharing rather than on co-ordination. It is very difficult to accept that the co-ordinator should have access to the Government at a high level in order to impose co-ordination, which is inevitably affected by the policy decisions of Governments as to priorities.

The claim, therefore, in *National Information Policy*, that NATIS committees responsible for a co-ordinating role would have "a semi-judicial function" and that they should be executive and "not be subservient to any minister or Government department" must be questioned. Analysis of some of the low-level functions suggested for NATIS in this policy statement does little to support the concept that the NATIS committees should be outside the normal administrative controls for specialized agencies.

The examples quoted of the reasons for the failure to achieve the free flow of information are low-level statements of widely accepted failures in many libraries; failure of the user to appreciate the nature of his problem; lack of know-how and appropriate guides; failure of the potential user to approach the appropriate staff; lack of suitable staff to assist user; the appropriate documents not being readily available; ignorance of the resources of other services; limitation of access to appropriate services; lack of adequate guides to documentation. All of these needs could be most effectively met by the provision of more resources or by voluntary co-operation between Government agencies, reinforced by some machinery to allocate special resources for approved purposes which could readily be the responsibility of the experts in this area—the staff of the Treasury.

The paper on *Design and Planning of National Information Systems* is, like *National Information Policy*, of value in stressing the importance of the free flow of information and in pointing out remedies for deficiencies, but is less successful in specific proposals. If the authors of the planning papers were not able to be more specific in their claims for the supreme importance of information, it is not surprising that member Governments became quickly as disillusioned with NATIS as they had been with UNISIST.

The *Design and Planning of National Information Systems* set out the objectives for national and international action under the NATIS programmes:

Formulation of a national information policy.

Design and planning of national information systems.

Methodology of analysis of users' needs and inventory of existing information sources.

Establishment of a legislative framework for the implementation of NATIS.

Methodology of cost analysis for the effective implementation of the national plan for NATIS in the context of its contribution to national development.

Design and Planning of National Information Systems was aimed at Government planners and indicated that "no single model could be designed for all countries", that "the formulation of broad information objectives must remain in the hands of Government departments", but a central co-ordinating unit should "establish the plan, acquire the resources, distribute responsibilities, and make arrangements for international liaison on the Governmental level. It would not be expected to carry out operational activities".

In spite of this last statements, the paper proceeded to quite a few appropriate examples, including the British Library Board, but this had very wide operational activities which were one reason for its success. Indeed, in my view, it is essential for focal points to have wide operational responsibilities if they are to be successful. They need to demonstrate to their more powerful sister institutions that they can provide worth-while services in exchange for the assistance required from them to meet national needs. The elements of the infrastructure were set out in Design and Planning of National Information Systems: libraries, documentation centers, Government information services, societies, and the publishing and printing industry. A little realism is interjected: "the very concept that the objective of NATIS is to encourage all services involved in the provision of information services for all sectors of the community and for all categories of users creates problems which can only be approached in a pragmatic or heuristic manner, as no one has yet seen or planned such a system".

Yet the Australian National Library had published by 1976 not only the basic planning volume Development of Resource Sharing Networks in the Framework of UNISIST (World Science Information System), NATIS (National Information Systems), and ALBIS (Australian Library Based Information System) which identified the priority networks and the participating bodies, but also detailed network studies for medical sciences, industry, and a national shared cataloguing network, which were in process of implementation. This was achieved in the only way in which it could be achieved—by voluntary co-operation with and support by much more powerful organisations than the National Library.

It is unrealistic, as Bowen Dees inferred on the basis of US experience, to consider establishing a co-ordinating body for scientific and technical information, much of which must remain confidential, and to equip it with powers to coerce other agencies. A Cabinet Committee passed a resolution in Canada several years ago for the transfer of the Canadian Institute of Scientific and Technical Information (CISTI) to the National Library of Canada. Support was, however, not given to the proposal by the Canadian Science Council, which controlled CISTI. Hence the transfer has not taken place and is not likely to take place in my view unless the National Library of Canada is able to demonstrate to the National Science Council that it will not only continue to receive services comparable to those of CISTI, but will also benefit from other improvements of services to the nation as a whole.

The Design and Planning of National Information Systems achieved, however, as much as could be expected in setting out a conceptual framework and stressing that there would inevitably be national divergencies arising from national circumstances. The functions of the sub-systems are set out clearly in the study: determine national needs and priorities for information; exploit by modern methods the possibilities of drawing on the world's store of knowledge; obtain such access by suitable investment in information/computer/telecommunication systems; strengthen Governmental and non-governmental information and communications systems; encourage manpower and educational programmes; draw up guidelines for the interface of the information sub-systems with libraries and archives. It is pertinent to note that NATIS guidelines also included Establishing a Legislative Framework for the Implementation of NATIS. The purpose of the proposed legislation was to add to, amend or apply existing legislation so as to create a statutory framework for implementing a national information policy by establishing the principle of a national information system providing for the planned development of library, documentation, and archive services; providing machinery for the implementation of plans and co-ordination; provision for resource allocation and the free flow of information; machinery for standards; facilities for the production and distribution of books and other materials required for information services; provision of the necessary computer and telecommunications facilities; of machinery for checking the accuracy and preserving the confidentiality of material in data banks; of education and training; determining the status and conditions of service of personnel; recognition of appropriate professional associations; regulation of qualifications; and provision for the inclusion of information personnel in manpower planning. The theoretical basis for NATIS has hardly been set out and the process of recognizing focal points had hardly been started, when yet another international information programme emerged—UNESCO's GIP, replacing NATIS.

UNESCO's General Information Programme (GIP)

The GIP arose as a result of the decision of UNESCO in 1976 to integrate its Culture and Communication Sectors. As a result of this reorganization, Member States replaced their NATIS committees by committees for the GIP, which included programmes relating not only to culture but also to communications. As a result membership of the General Information Committee was wider than that of the NATIS committees, which, in their turn, had been wider than the UNISIST committees.

The activities of the GIP committees were inevitably largely concerned with the co-ordination of a wide range of services, which had few operational points in common. Hence the committees became more and more separated from reality and concentrated on an unproductive planning exercise. Nevertheless, the Director General of UNESCO claimed subsequently that "the process of integration, which had been under way for more than two years, had begun to produce appreciable results in regard to co-ordination". Yet a further stage in the planning programme was envisaged with a view to co-ordinating more effectively not only the execution of the programme but also its actual formation.

New World Information and Communication Order (NWIO)

The 19th session of the UNESCO General Conference call for yet another information organization—a New World Information and Communication Order. This arose from the alleged discovery that "many disparate parts of the UNESCO programme, for example the communication sector, science policy information, General Information Programme had a common core". The 20th session of the UNESCO General Conference endorsed "efforts to establish a new, more just and more balanced world information and communication order". The Director General of UNESCO was invited "within the limits of the Programme and Budget approved by the General Conference 1979-80...to continue his efforts with a view to the establishment" of this new order, entailing in particular the promotion of national systems in developing countries and the establishment of a new equilibrium and greater reciprocity in the information flow.

To conclude, it may be surmised, national libraries and similar practical institutions had also recognized the need to promote a better flow of information. An account of their more pragmatic activities is contained in subsequent chapters. But there is no doubt that the successive schemes of UNESCO to promote the formulation and implementation of international and national information policies had provided the essential framework within which some modest progress has been achieved during the last decade and the planning process continues. Let us wait for further fruitful development.

8

Issue of Other Electronic Library Materials

"The Internet has the potential to change radically much of our work, whether it be as reference specialists or as recommending officers". Today that statement might best be phrased as "The Internet *has* radically changed ..." Libraries are making ever-increasing use of Internet resources in their service programs and as part of their "virtual collections". Certainly the electronic environment goes well beyond just Internet/Web resources, but those resources are becoming more and more dominant factors.

A question often asked is: Are electronic materials merely another type of storage medium, like microforms? They are, indeed, another storage format in one sense, because digitized data does allow compact storage of large quantities of information. However, digital formats also allow data manipulation in ways that are not cost-effective in other formats. Further, the electronic environment allows both free-text and Boolean searching.

Downloading information from electronic resources to a user's computer and being able to cut, paste, move, add and delete as much as desired is now possible. This is possible either with or without complying with copyright;

the new copyright law has special implication for libraries. Such capabilities make electronic information the preferred information format for many users. Electronic formats cause libraries and information centers to concentrate their attention on overall operations and rethink systems and services in a way never before required. To some degree, it may be a question of the survival of our field. Electronic information producers can deliver the product directly to the end user at home or in the office and increasingly they are doing so.

Proper planning, realistic goals and intelligent reorganization of operations will ensure that libraries play an ever-expanding role in the information transfer process in the electronic age. Electronic delivery of information requires delivery platforms, equipment, software, substantial user support and time to assess the various services and products that producers offer. Few users have the time, energy, inclination, or funds to handle all these activities effectively. Libraries can and should undertake these tasks. If we do not, someone else will.

The electronic environment creates several dichotomies for libraries and information centers: print versus electronic; ownership versus access; user need versus institutional need; free versus fee; and gatekeeper versus user selection. It is not a matter of either/or; rather, it is a matter of determining the proper local mix. Clearly, one cannot make the necessary judgments about these issues without knowing the local users, what information they want and need, how and where they use the information, what type of equipment they have, what network capabilities exist and what monetary and equipment resources are available to the library or information center. Print and electronic information sources are both complementary and competitive. Users with an interest in historical information and data certainly will require, in most cases, collections of older print material. Few of the electronic products or services provide pre-1970s information. This may change in time, but at the moment recent information, is in highest demand and it is on the highest-demand areas that commercial providers focus. (One example of a change in backfile access is JSTOR; however, it is worth noting that this is a library-initiated rather than commercially run project).

One obvious advantage of print sources is that they do not malfunction and one can use them in a variety of locations without having to consider power, network connections and similar technical issues. However, electronic sources have a clear advantage in terms of locating and manipulating information. In any case, it is imperative to have an understanding of the service community's preferences for end users of print and electronic information. Traditionally, libraries and information centers depended on an ownership-of-materials model as the primary means of meeting customer information needs. Interlibrary loans (ILL) for books and photocopies of journal articles more or less filled any gaps between the local collections and local needs. Interlibrary loan adheres to the ownership-of-materials model in that it requires other libraries to own the loaned material. Customers check out ILL materials from their home library and return the materials to the local library when finished; the local library then ships the materials back to the lending source.

For all practical purposes, this system operates as if the local library owned the items. Another form of ownership is photocopied ILL journal articles that the user gets to keep.

The ILL process is slow, but it preserves the sense of ownership. Taking the ownership model to an extreme, research libraries once attempted to acquire everything their service community actually did or might need: the goals were impossible to achieve and the attempt was costly. Even in a cooperative collection environment, it was not possible for libraries to own everything their customers wanted or might conceivably want. Electronic materials and methods of information dissemination present the opportunity for libraries and information centers to provide access to more resources than they can realistically expect to acquire and house. Access can be directed to a user's home or workplace, allowing end users to make independent choices about what they want, from what source and how quickly. Access may be a more cost-effective option for the library or information center, even if the organization pays for all searches and documents ordered.

In fact, balancing of individual and institutional needs raises the issue of free versus fee services. There is the long-standing tradition of free library service. Though maintaining this tradition is the goal of many information professionals, it has been some time since all services were free. Charging for services began with charging for photocopying and the practice has expanded steadily over the years.

In the electronic environment, it is easy to associate service costs with individual customers and there are a greater variety of costs. Because it is easier to associate costs with an individual in the electronic environment than it is in the print environment, it is possible to pass the charges on to the customer. To some degree, the new costs are not new; they were merely hidden or too time-consuming to track in the print world. Again, how far one goes in charging fees depends on the local situation and service community.

Notably, libraries supporting educational programs are more likely to absorb the costs for electronic information that directly supports instruction and pass on charges for noninstructional uses. Some institutions, like Loyola Marymount University, have a sliding scale, allowing for a base level of free access and some form of cost sharing as the individual's use increases. Public libraries must consider the economic differences in the community with the goal of assuring that those who cannot afford to pay the fees do not become information-poor.

Special libraries may pass costs to project teams or departments to answer an organization's desire to track actual operating costs of various units; in other situations, the costs are considered overhead and are not assigned to any unit other than the information center. The roles of the library, computing services, telecommunication services and customers in electronic information transfer is a topic of debate in electronic discussion groups and conferences, as well as in the literature and in the institution. Who has primary responsibility? If shared, how is it shared? Who decides what will be available? Who supports and maintains the service(s)? None of these questions, nor many related ones, have clear answers. We are in the process of developing models based on experience. Efforts to merge the various institutional players have not proven successful.

However, as noted in chapter 1, it is clear that text, numeric, voice and image data technologies are becoming integrated and, at some point, the institution must come to grips with the need to coordinate the various activities. One aspect of the debate is whether there should be preselection of electronic materials. In preselection, the library or information center plays the role of gatekeeper, rather than letting users search independently. Although the terms are different, the fundamental issue is as old as libraries and collection development.

Years ago, a favorite examination question in collection development courses was, "Is collection development selection or censorship?" On one side are those who believe that no one should predetermine what resources best fit the organization's mission and profile. Their position is, let the user find what she or he needs without preselection by someone else. The opposite view is that preselection and guidance are in the best interests of both the users and the organization.

As in the past, libraries, information centers and organizations cannot provide access to everything. Thus, choices are inevitable; someone or some group must function as a gatekeeper or, at least, as a cost controller.

Refusing to perform the gatekeeper function is akin to putting a person in the middle of a multimillion-volume storehouse, with only a floor plan keyed to broad classification groupings and saying to this person, "You are on your own". That will waste not only the individual's time, but also the institution's resources. In a sense, this view is a return to the research library philosophy of the 1950s, 1960s and early 1970s: "Get everything possible, just in case". A gatekeeper who points the way to potentially useful materials, perhaps by adding pointers on the library's Web home page, aids the user in the long run and maximizes the benefit of the institution's funding for information services. When the library or information center provides such assistance, it does not deny the user access to other electronic resources available through other services, such as the Internet (assuming the individual has network access and the ability to explore it effectively).

One advantage of electronic collection building, compared with building print collections, is more effective tracking of the person using the information and what resources she or he used that one could supply with electronic materials. (Although state-of-the-art online circulation systems allow one to easily get similar information about circulated items, for in-house use the best one can do is track the items used, not who used them). Many of the better commercial electronic products have management report software that allows one to learn how and when the users accessed the material. One gets more accurate and complete data with less effort in the electronic environment.

It is up to librarians to make effective use of the data to provide the right information at the right time at the right cost.

Issues in Electronic Collection Building

One issue that makes processing some e-materials, especially Web/ Internet materials, challenging is that they do not usually remain "fixed" in the way print materials do. Anyone with any amount of experience with Web/Internet materials has at least once encountered a message indicating that the URL one bookmarked is no longer operative. Sometimes a new address is provided on a "transition page", but often there is no referring link. Not only are addresses variable, but so is the content of the site. "This document last modified on ..." is a message found on many Internet/ Web sites; another message is "under construction". Both messages make it clear that what you see today may not be what or all you will see tomorrow.

Some individuals believe that, as we stated in the opening paragraph of this chapter, electronic materials and the Internet have indeed radically changed collection development.

Kathleen Kluegel wrote, "it is time to see if the traditional models of technical processes, collection development and collection management still fit the needs of the library and its users".

Certainly she is correct that electronic resources require different cataloging processing. The basic question, though, is whether they are really so different as to require radical changes in processing activities. The fact that libraries are leasing or renting the data does not really change the acquisition process. Certainly there are echoes of the old approval plan in the free trial that many e-material vendors generally offer.

An aspect of e-materials that is seldom addressed is how to deal with bytes rather than books. This is an area where we *do* need to make radical changes in how we deal with collection statistics. Many agencies that collect data about libraries do not ask about electronic resources—in some cases they only ask about "volumes". Volumes are also something funding bodies understand; they can see and hold them.

The fact that one "rents" rather than owns the material, at least in many instances, also raises questions in funders' mind about what they and the library have to show for expending substantial amounts of money on e-materials. With packages of e-materials, the vendors and producers decide what is or is not included, as well as for how long. It is not uncommon for packages' content to change even during a single lease period. That, of course, raises the question of what to count. For example, is a package such as First Search one package or N number of databases? If one counted just the packages, one could not compare libraries very accurately, bec-ause libraries can turn off access to individual databases. Why do that? Because the OCLC pricing model is per-search-based; libraries can and do turn off databases that are least useful to local users but may generate a significant number of searches.

In the past, library "status" was, at least in part, a function of the size of collection—the more volumes, the higher the status. Changeable packages make for variable counts, assuming that one counts databases and create fluctuating statistics that are difficult to quickly explain to nonlibrarians. When adding a printed item into one's OPAC, one has a reasonable expectation that the only time a change to the record will be needed is if the item is withdrawn.

The lack of a "final" contact, if one adds a record for an electronic product to the OPAC, means either that someone must check the site on a regular basis and make any needed adjustments in the OPAC record, or that the library must accept the fact many such records no longer reflect reality. Although it is possible to "automate" the process of checking links, it still requires people power to check content, make decisions about any needed changes, and input the new information.

Types of Electronic Materials

Of the major type of electronic resources, at present full text is the most challenging and replete with options. We covered the issues of e-serials. Here we will just remind readers there are two categories—electronic only and electronic/print—of interest in this chapter. E-only journals present a decision point: the library must decide how to provide access (that is, through the library or other gatekeeper or gateway or through direct access).

It also must decide whether to include a record of those titles in its OPAC. Certainly the technical, legal, and financial issues addressed later in this chapter must be considered, but collection development issues are easily dealt with.

Full-text material comes in three formats: online, CD-ROM and print. In some cases, there are cost differences when both print and electronic formats are available. As we mentioned, the vendor or publisher frequently has one price for the print version and a different price for the electronic version. If one orders just the electronic version, there is a third price, roughly equal to the sum of the print and electronic rates. An advantage to having both formats becomes obvious during, for example, a power outage when users still have access to the print version. Another question is the definition of *full text.* Often, in the online version, it means text without graphics. As of 1999, online databases offered some limited graphical interfaces and imaged information. The reason for the limits is that images, (charts, tables, and other illustrations(require substantial amounts of disk space and delivery time, as well as delivery platforms capable of handling images.

CD-ROMs, in contrast, provide a wide range of imaging area, including full-motion video. Windows interfaces, now available with many CD-ROM products, will probably be available soon for online services. Graphics require megabytes of memory and powerful PCs (currently, mid- to high-end Pentiums), more powerful than many PC owners own. In addition, even if an end user's modem is capable of transmitting data at 56KB, online imaging is a slow process.

Because of imaging issues, it will probably be some

time before online services follow in the footsteps of OCLS's *Clinical Trials* journal. Although we devoted an entire chapter to e-serials, we also need to give some attention to e-books. WE opened this edition with a brief discussion of the controversy surrounding the 1998 Booker award and the question of "when is a book a bok." Just as there are variation in e-serials, so there are with e-books. Some, like Patricia le Roy's *Angels of Russia,* are available only in an electronic version. One Website for e-books is "Alex: A catalog of Electronic Books on the Internet" (<http://ww.lib.ncsu.edu/whatsnew/index.htm#e book>).

One of the oldest efforts in digitizing existing books is Project Gutenberg. A goal of that Project is to have 10,000 titles available in its "Project Gutenberg Electronic Public Library" (<http:..promo.net/pg>). Titles in the project are all public domain (no longer covered by copyright) items. AT a different level, the Oxford Text Archives is primary interest to academics. The Archives contains about 2,000 literary works as well as collections of unpublished field notes of linguists. This is a noncommercial service available to scholars to archive their electronic texts (<http:..firth.natcorp.ox.ac.uk/ota/public/index.shtml>).

Other projects include the University of Michigan Libraries' "UM Press" (<http://www.press.umich.edu/<), and the School of Library and Information Studies' "Humanities Text Initiative" (<http://www.hti.umich.eda>), which focuses on Middle English materials and American poetry, as well as recent releases from the UM Press. From Brown University there is "The Woman Writers Project" (<http://www.brown.edu?). This project' goal is to create a full-text database of the publications in English written by women between 1330 and 1830. Since 1992, the "Electronic Text Center at the University of Virginia (<http://extext.lib.virginia.edu>)

has been working to create a unique collection of online materials. By early 1999, the collection included "45,000 on- and off-line humanities texts in twelve languages with more than 50,000 related images (book illustrations, covers, manuscripts, newspaper pages, images of Special Collections books, museum objects, etc.)."

With any full-text material, whether book for serial, one issue to consider is the way the text was digitized: ASCII, Adobe, HTML, or SGHL. ASCII is the oldest and in many ways the easiest approach. However, one loses most of the formatting of the original document, as well as any images,. Adobe Acrobat PDF (Portable Documentary Format) is an approach that retains formatting and images and is frequently encountered on the Internet. HTML (Hypertext Markup Language) is probably the most common method used on the World Wide Web. It is in fact a sub-language of SGML (Standard Generalized Markup Language). Many organizations use SGML to digitize their internal documents. There are several advantages of using SGML; it is an international standard, it is device independent and it is system independent. Having documents in SGML makes it easier to change systems without incurring significant document conversion costs.

Music

Music, in recorded form, is available on the Internet, but almost nothing exists for musical scores. The only site of which we are aware is Stanford University's Center for Computer Assisted Research in the Humanities (<http://musedata-stanford.edu>) and there are fees to access the material. This site does have full electronic scores of many of the classical works. A controversy was brewing in early 1999 regarding the availability of MP3 files.

This compression format allows for digitization and

copying of music files, which are easily posted on the Internet, rarely legally. In February 1999, Leonardo Chiariglione, who invented the format, was named to head the "Secure Digital Music Initiative" to standardize the way songs and albums are distributed on the Internet. This is obviously an issue that concerns the music industry and until the issue can be addressed, one's best bet to find legal recordings is at recording company sites.

Numeric Databases

Numeric databases have been part of library or information center collecting activities for at least 25 years. Generally, libraries acquired these data sets, such as the U.S. Census, as tapes that were mounted on a mainframe. Today, researchers can gain access to such sets online. A disadvantage is that downloading large data sets takes a long time; an advantage is that local ownership speeds the work. A source for numeric data sets is the Inter-University Consortium for Political and Social Research (ICPSR) at the University of Michigan (<http://www.icpsr.umich.edu>). Hundreds of universities in 22 countries around the world are members of ICPSR. This consortium serves as a central repository and dissemination service for social science electronic data sets.

Since its establishment in the early 1960s, ICPSR has collected data sets that cover a broad range of topics. Beginning with a few major surveys of the American electorate, the holdings of the archive have now broadened to include comparable information from diverse settings and for extended periods. Data ranging from nineteenth-century French census materials to recent sessions of the United Nations, from American elections in the 1790s to the socioeconomic structure of Polish *poviats,* from characteristics of Knights of Labor Assemblies to expectations of American consumers, are contained in the archive. When considering numeric collection building, one must remember that these tend to be very large files and format or compatibility may be issues to consider, as well as the quality of the documentation.

In the case of ICPSR, data sets are available as round tapes, 9-track, or diskettes. It is also possible to FTP files online using CD Net (Consortium Data Network) on the Internet. Users electing this mode might pay telecommunication charges, as well as University of Michigan computer services charges. Though avoiding the potential conversion costs, the online approach leaves open the possibility of surprisingly large and unpredictable service and telecommunication charges. Occasionally, one may encounter a conflict between how long users wish to have access to the data and how long the organization's computing service is willing to make the tapes accessible through the campus network. This may result in pressure on the library not only to acquire the data sets, but also to have in-house CPU capacity to operate statistical software packages, as well as mount the tapes. Support depends both on people with the skills and knowledge to do the technical work and on sound documen-tation. Anyone who has seen the documentation that accompanies many commercial products can imagine the quality of documentation for data sets from researchers whose primary purpose was their own project. If the library is already mounting bibliographic or full-text tapes, it may have staff with appropriate computer operations background.

Probably, however, the staff will not have experience with all the various statistical packages on the market (such as SPSS and SAS). Support means institutional costs. Again, there are costs associated with either mode of access (online or tape). Careful consideration of both options and how to handle the charges is essential before moving into the business of acquiring data sets.

Software

Few libraries actively collect software because of copyright problems and the difficulty of maintaining the integrity of the software. Though it is possible to collect operating systems, few, if any, libraries maintain collections of these programs for public use. Programming tools and languages are two other types of software that are rarely collected. The two areas where some collecting occurs are applications and, as discussed earlier, data files. Libraries are acquiring more and more books that come with software that is integral to use of the printed material. School media centers, if they have responsibility for computing services, are the most likely to maintain collections of educational application programs. (Perhaps the safest software to collect is so-called shareware).

Without a doubt, libraries and collection development officers will face increasing pressure to add electronic formats. Cost, legal and selection issues each will become more complex as time goes by. Balancing the various needs will present challenges for all concerned.

Selection Issues

Loyola Marymount University considers four broad categories of issues when evaluating a new electronic product: content, access, support and cost. The approach is similar to what other libraries do in this area (see fig. 8.1, pp. 217-19).

Content

As with any format, content issues should be the first consideration. There is some temptation to acquire an electronic format because it is new, because others have it, because it is attractive or entertaining, because it is multimedia-based, or because it will interface with existing equipment. None of these are valid reasons for adding a title. Instead, care should be taken to make certain the item matches up with both library and institutional goals. In an ideal situation, the item will match several goals.

Though popularity, or high demand, is a basic reason for selecting an item, it also creates some public service concerns. One can lease or buy multiple copies of bestseller books, develop request lists and have a few rental copies of high-demand items. Few libraries or information centers circulate their journals, which usually means that current journals are available when a user seeks them. A single-user license for a CD-ROM product, however, can create queues and substantial paper and ink/toner costs (if there is a printer attached to the computer) as well as a need for equipment maintenance of heavily used hardware. Thus, though multiple users are an important factor in the selection decision, the consequences of that popularity also must be taken into account. A popular item may require purchasing a multiple-user license or several single-user copies to handle the workload. All these options add to the cost. Content of the product is the key issue, as it is for any addition to the collection. If the product is bibliographic or statistical in nature, one must consider how far back in time the data goes. What use characteristics of the subject field are represented in the product? The myth that older literature in the sciences is obsolete has little research documentation. Though it is true of all fields that use declines with age, that does not mean that use, or importance to the field, ceases entirely.

Understanding local use patterns will be a key issue in making the selection decision. More and more full-text and image CD-ROMs are spin-offs of print publications. Some of the products incorporate only a portion of the print version, but others contain everything. The question is,

"How complete or comprehensive is the product?" Here's a rough rule of thumb: if the price is less than $200, chances are it is not the full print version, especially if there are extensive graphics in the print edition. In addition to these questions, there are other considerations. For instance, how often is the product updated? Are there plans to add to the back-files? If so, how soon will they be added and how far back will they go? These are key questions for products that incorporate bibliographic and abstracting data.

Occasionally vendors advertise greater coverage than the product actually offers. In 1992, Loyola Marymount University reviewed the initial offering of a bibliographic CD-ROM product that claimed coverage from 1520 to 1990. The search data capabilities were used to check the number of items included for several sets of years (1986 to 1990 and 1520 to 1526) and the results were surprising. There were more items for the sixteenth century than for the most recent. In fact, there were an equal number of items for 1520 and 1990. By checking 1989 and 1990 issues of a quarterly journal covered by the database, it became clear that there was only limited coverage of the late 1980s and 1990s. Indexing of that particular journal ended in mid-1989. The producers did have 93 items from 1990 in the database, so the claim of coverage from 1520 to 1990 was not exactly false. Nevertheless, it was not completely accurate either, because there were at least 1,000 items from 1990 that should have been in the database.

The annual updates to the product would have improved coverage of the most recent five-year period, but would not cover the most recent years, if the first offering was indicative of future indexing practices. Problems like this make it important to seek out reviews *and* require at least a 30 day trial for new products. Clearly, the public service staff will need to be fully aware of the various product limitations, so that they can make the end users equally aware of the situation. This is one excellent reason why library and information center staffs need to continue to serve as interpreters and guides to information services, whether electronic or print. In selecting any product for the collection, aspects like quality, accuracy, authoritativeness and currency of data are factors any collection development officer will consider. With electronic products, these factors can be even more significant than with other formats.

Many people have great respect for anything in print and transfer that faith to electronic products, which they believe always contain the most current, complete and accurate information available. This almost-blind end-user acceptance of electronic information means that selection personnel must be careful in their decisions about electronic formats.

As mentioned previously, long-term availability is another concern. Online material sometimes disappears overnight. The person operating a discussion list or Website may simply stop maintaining the service, or may make a significant change in a server; some users don't learn of the change and they lose that connection. With a print version in the collection, there is a reasonable degree of certainty that the data will always be available, as long as the book remains a part of the collection.

A real concern is how long the CD-ROM format will be with us. Will full text on CD-ROM become the next "problem" format, rather like sound recordings? How many times must a library or information center acquire the same information?

Will *Time* become available on multiple formats, like the sound recordings of Handel's *Water Music—first* a 78-rpm disk, then a 33 1/3-rpm disk, then 8-track tape, then cassette and now CD and MP3? If one of the library's or information center's goals is to preserve information for future generations, then format viability and support must be a concern. Technologists claim there is nothing to worry about. They say once the information is digitized it can be preserved. What is to say that digitization is the final process? Will systems 50 years in the future have the capability to handle "ancient" material in an ASCII format?

More to the point, who will own that data and what will it cost to have access? These questions have no ready answers. We do know that print has served humankind very well for centuries and that it can continue to do so without regard to operating systems or hardware delivery platforms. A final item on the list of content considerations is whether the product offers some value-added advantage over existing print versions.

Especially important is any type of customization the producer offers that more closely links the product's content to the local collections. For example, indexes that are customized to show which indexed titles are locally available would have added value. Almost all electronic products offer easier searching, more search options and generally faster results than their print counterparts. Because of this, it is important to try to find some other value-added feature before committing funds. As Matthew Ciolek suggested, a danger exists that electronic material, especially on the Web, will move from WWW to MMM (Multi-Media Mediocrity).

Access

Being able to customize a product to indicate local

holdings brings us to the second major category of selection issues: *access.* One aspect of access is availability of materials. This issue applies primarily to the indexing, abstracting and table of contents products. As noted in chapter 6, when the library adds a new indexing or abstracting service, users will see citations to some publications that are not in the local collection. A decision to give users access to the tables of contents of thousands of periodicals will, for most libraries, generate numerous requests for articles from titles not available locally. One should not ignore the impact on ILL service when making this decision. Returning to other access issues, one question that requires an answer is: how compatible is the product with the local network or library automation system? Related to compatibility is the question of licensing; that is, what is the difference in cost between single-user and multiple-user or networking licenses?

Also of concern is the type of search engine or interface used by the product. One must consider how different it is from other electronic products already locally available. In the past, one could assume Boolean logic searching, but today some vendors are using statistical searching or weighted terms. (*Weighted term searching* is a system that retrieves on the basis of word-frequency matches of search terms to words in the document and presents the user with the most frequent matches first). The popularity of the latter system in commercial text imaging and retrieval systems (for example, a records management application) is causing companies like Westlaw and Mead Data Central to use statistical searching engines. Strategies for a successful search are very different for the two search engines.

This will translate into extra training for staff and patrons alike. The overarching access issue is the user.

Where (library, office, home), when (during library operating hours, 24 hours per day) and how (local network, Internet, commercial service) does the end user gain access to the information? As a general rule, as accessibility goes up, so does the cost. An as-yet-unavailable ideal solution is having everything available 24 hours a day, from any authorized location, with full cost control capability and no need for local support.

Support should be a prime consideration during the selection process. How much training does a user need to successfully use the product? Having only similar products, or having only a few variations in how one can use products, means that the public service staff will have less support activity.

This leads to another question: how much initial and ongoing staff training is necessary to provide customer support? The answers to these questions depend on the quality of the documentation that accompanies the product. Usually, a toll-free telephone number for vendor support works well only when the caller has good to fair technical knowledge of the product.

Usually, this means that staff members rather than end users must make the call. Anyone with public service experience knows that most people follow the directions only when everything else fails. Reading introductory material about how to use print resources was never a strong point with general users. They are no more likely to take the time to read instructions for electronic products, some of which come with extensive user manuals.

A rule of thumb is: the bigger the manual, the more help the public service staff will have to provide. Information about ease of use and size or usefulness of manuals may appear in product reviews (if a review can be found). Some review sources to consult are *Database: Magazine of Electronic Database Reviews, Online and CD-ROM Review* and *American Reference Books Annual (ARBA)*. Often, information about ease of use and size of the manual is available only after the library receives the product.

Now, questions about vendor/producer reliability are important support considerations. Reliability of the producer is a more significant issue with electronic products than it is with print products. Will the toll-free telephone number for customer help remain active and is help available at times when it would likely be needed? What are the systems (computing resource) requirements? Will new versions result in retraining users or reconfiguring the local system? What is the relationship between vendor support service hours and the library's hours? Just because the producer of the electronic product is one the library staff knows from its nonelectronic products does not mean that the transition to the new format will be smooth. It also does not mean that the producer will stay with the format or support existing products if the company decides to drop the format. Just as technology changes rapidly, so do the producers of electronic materials. Some software can be unreliable and troublesome. Invariably, some products have one or more bugs that take time and effort to eliminate. A few seem to have bugs in each new release, although, in a sense, this is better than the occasional bug.

When there is a consistent pattern, one can plan how to do the debugging, instead of encountering unexpected problems. Compatibility of hardware and software is also a key issue in selecting a format for mounting electronic information. Support issues affect the impact new products have on existing services and activities. Some new products reduce pressure on the staff (for example, the full text of materials frequently requested through ILL).

In some instances, it may be possible to reduce staff work by giving end users thorough training in using a product and assigning users their own accounts and passwords. Other times, there will be a substantial increase in the staff workload. In those cases, staff discussions about the impact and the value of the product are an essential part of the decision-making process.

There are a variety of Websites that are useful to collection development officers. A very good article on this area is by Shelley Mien and her colleagues.

A starting point for anyone interested in collection management is the COLLDV-L@usc.edu discussion list. Another source is the Internet, where most major publishers as well as vendors and suppliers have Websites. Examples are the Yankee Book Peddler (<http://www.ybp.com>) and EBSCO (<http://www.ebsco.com>). Generally, these sites are digitized versions of the catalogs and promotional materials that one can secure in a paper format. What one usually gains from looking at the Websites is the most current pricing information, as well as information about recent releases or new services. Something akin to the print version of *Publisher's Trade List Annual* is a site maintained by Northern Lights Internet Solutions, titled "Publisher's Catalogs Home Page" (<httpl/www.lights.com/ publisher>). Obviously, the ability to go to one site to access multiple publisher catalogs can save selection staff time. Probably the most comprehensive site for acquisitions is AcqWeb, maintained by the staff at the Vanderbilt Law School Library (<http://www. library.vanderbilt.edu/law/ acqs/acqs.html>). This site also has an excellent directory of publishers and vendors. We mentioned a number of sites to consult for serials in chapter 7; however, we wish to note here our favorite serials site: <http:lltoltec.lib.utk.edu/ —serials/sertools.htm>. For government documents, a good starting point is GPO Access (<http//www.access.gpo.gov/ su_docs/ db2.html>).

Many types of libraries use reviews in their selection processes. A useful site for schools and public libraries is *Booklist* (<http://www.ala.org/booklist/ index.html>);a notable addition in the electronic version, not available in the print edition, is a cumulative index to its reviews. One interesting site of special interest to public libraries is "Chapter One" (<httpl/www.dialabook.inter. net>), which provides the full text of the first chapter as well as the table of contexts for the titles covered. Selectors can also locate book reviews published in many U.S. newspapers: for example, *New York Times Book Review* (<http://www.nytimes.com/>), which requires user registration to gain access to this file; or *Los Angeles Times Book Review,* which has free access (<http:/ /www.latimes.com/HOME/NEWS/BOOKS>).

Additional cost considerations for one or more electronic formats may include connection and telecommunication charges; display or print charges; downloading charges; customization charges; optional features, such as saved searches; and charges for management reports or software. Even CD-ROM products have imposed printing charges; for example, UMI's full-text CD-ROM *Business Periodicals Ondisc* (BPO) imposed a 10-percent royalty charge for each page printed. This leads to a very pertinent question: when you buy a CD-ROM product, what do you *buy?* Do you own the material, or do you own only a license to use the material for a period of time? If equipment is included as part of the contract, does it revert to the library after a stated number of years, or must it be returned when and if the subscription is cancelled? Is a service contract available for this equipment? If so, is the cost of this less than an independent service contract that the library might purchase? The answers vary by product and vendor. In the past, libraries did not send back quarterly issues of print indexing services when the annual volume arrived. However, with most CD-ROM indexing products, the library only leases the product and must return superseded discs or make a cut in the edge of the disk to prevent use. This is the route staff at the Northern Virginia Community College Alexandria Campus Library had to take when they cancelled their subscription to the CD-ROM version of *Pro Quest Direct.* Staff had to destroy more than 500 individual discs and send an affidavit to UMI after this was done. Occasionally, the library can arrange to continue to use the earlier discs in another area of the library. For example, technical services might use the current version of *BIP* while reference uses the preceding version. With a paper subscription, the library retains all the paper copies after cancelling the subscription; with a CD-ROM subscription, the library may have nothing to show for its investment after it cancels the service.

In addition to vendor costs, local costs are a factor in the decision-making process. The computers and other hardware required to use electronic materials are generally more expensive to buy and maintain than other media playback equipment. As programmable units, they are susceptible to system failure, to loss of information because of power fluctuations and inadvertent user error, to tampering by computer hackers, to viruses and to theft. All of these factors generate additional costs (equipment; security devices; service contracts and maintenance; and, all too often, replacement). An estimate of the amount of printing or downloading activity the product will generate is another cost factor that cannot be ignored. Even without a royalty fee, there are printing costs, assuming that the decision is to allow users to print information. Paper, ink, ribbon and toner cartridge costs can and do mount quickly, if there is no effort to control them. Libraries and information centers employ several techniques to control such costs. One obvious method is to assess a printing charge. (There are coin and debit-card units that work with printers). Another method is to allocate a number of free copies per user, with the staff providing the appropriate number of sheets of paper and charging for additional paper. This approach generates a cost in staff time to provide the paper and, occasionally, to put the paper into the printer or troubleshoot paper jams. Some libraries allow downloading to disk instead of printing. There are several drawbacks to this approach. First, the library must keep on hand a stock of disks to sell. Second, some products do not allow downloading. Another serious dis-advantage is that not all customers can use downloaded data, which means that the library *must* allow some printing or risk having a single user tie up a product for extended periods. Plus, allowing patrons to download opens the risk of them inserting a virus-infected disk into the computer—if arrangements have not been made to scan disks before use.

For popular products, libraries want to keep the customer turnover rate as high as possible, which means offering both printing and downloading. Shareware programs, such as PRNAFILE, provide a way of printing to disk rather than to paper, which is useful for programs that are not set up for downloading. Another method for handling printing costs is to locate a system printer, perhaps connected to a local area network, in a staff area, making it possible to monitor and charge for printing activities. This option generates staff costs but establishes a distribution system that assures that each customer gets the right printout.

If the institution is networked and has sophisticated software, printing charges, as well as other costs of use, could become automatic debits against individual user accounts. An additional option, which is becoming more and more popular for Web-based resources, is to e-mail articles to the patron's own account. This assumes that users have the capability to send and receive e-mail—but free options such as HotMail do exist. This can transfer printing costs to the individual user and save valuable library resources. In 1994, Peter Young stressed the need to create a paradigm for libraries and librarians, addressing the need to evaluate resources as quartifiable commodities and products. In that same year, a team of British researchers outlined a scenario in which information as a commodity was examined not only in terms of the set price of the commodity (such as an online database), but also in terms of the total cost of all the elements of an electronic resource. Karen Sevenningsen wrote a very good survey article on this topic and provided several models one can employ for conducting cost analysis.

Some More Issues

The legal, financial and technical issues relating to electronic acquisitions and processing work, as well as to other activities and services, are important enough to merit extra emphasis. One question that becomes increasingly important as one moves further and further into the arena of electronic collection development is how users know the material is available. Providing lists of possible Internet sites, with addresses, or even creating and maintaining a library Web page with direct links to the available resources, works reasonably well as long as the list is manageable and resources are available to create and maintain the Website. As the listing grows in length, grouping by subject is a frequent next step. In a sense, libraries begin to develop another online catalog, but why have two online catalogs?

OCLC began looking at Internet resources in 1991 and by 1993 was testing the suitability and usefulness of the MARC format and AACR2 for cataloging sites and materials found. By 1995, it was apparent that "traditional" cataloging systems would work for most Internet resources and that linking the catalog record to the resource site was highly desirable. After some discussion, the USMARC record added the 856 field (Electronic Location and Access). That field is now the location of URL (Uniform Resource Locator) information.

Erik Jul, in a 1997 article, noted that: "Cataloging Internet resources raises many critical questions, among which three stand out as fundamental: (1) Are Internet resources worth cataloging? (2) Is traditional MARC/ AACR2 cataloging appropriate for Internet resources? (3) What about resources that change location?" One might add to his last question the phrase "or that simply disappear?" Certainly it seems reasonable, since we employ cataloging methods for other information formats in our collections, that we do the same with Internet materials deemed appropriate for our service population.

Great difficulty arises in attempting to answer Jul's last question about changing (or disappearing) locations or resources. Anyone with even limited experience using Internet resources has encountered the message "Error 404, File Not Found" at least once. According to data from the OCLC Inter-Cat project, an average of 3 percent of URLs could note accessed during any given test. The time and effort necessary to check and update records are considerable.

There are products that can assist in checking URLs, but when there is a change in address for an item in the OPAC, someone has to make the required changes. One good Website for valuable Internet resources is the Internet Scout Project, which is funded by the National Science Foundation and operated by the Computer Science Department at the University of Wisconsin-Madison (<http://scout.cs.wisc.edu>). The Scout Report is prepared on a weekly basis and a daily "Net-Happenings" report is available via e-mail.

Besides the other issues we have addressed, there are legal issues involved in the use of electronic resources that cannot be ignored. These issues encompass both copyright and licensing agreements. Copyright involves several topics: fair use, preservation and production. Electronic (digital) material is easy to transmit, manipulate and duplicate. These features make the medium popular, but also raise copyright questions.

According to Mark McGuire:

> One of many challenges in the digital realm is the problem of ensuring appropriate compensation in transactions involving intellectual property. Other considerations include: ascertaining and proving liability in information malpractice; safeguarding information integrity; ensuring respect for privacy; and maintaining equitable access to information.

Achieving compliance with these copyright requirements and standards provides ongoing challenges for library and information center staffs. Some of the use issues are addressed by the licensing agreements accompanying the product or contract for online services. Rather like photocopying services, the library takes no responsibility for what users do with downloaded data after they leave the library. Whether posting signs regarding copyright in the electronic work area(s) will prove adequate to protect libraries and information centers remains to be seen. In any case, the staff must know what use rights exist for each product. The entire question of preserving print material by converting it to a digital format is slowly being resolved. In all likelihood, if the digital material is not publicly accessible, except through the group preserving the material, that will be acceptable to everyone. The ease with which electronic data is manipulated and duplicated is one of the concerns regarding preservation of materials that are becoming too brittle or fragile to handle.

A complex area is that of author responsibility or ownership. Perhaps the idea put forward by McGuire, or something similar—embedding codes in the data to link various information elements to their original producers, thus identifying authorship as well as assigning responsibility for content—will solve the problem.

In addition, such coding could ensure that economic value is equitably attributed to the originators. Such a system would avoid the fair use concerns that Robert Cost identified as the key problem: "We have lost the control necessary for copyright law to be effective. Control over copies is hopeless".

When the library or information center provides equipment or assists with multimedia production, under copyright law, it has some responsibility for assuring that the copied material is public domain or that permission is granted to reproduce the material.

Copyright law requires libraries and information centers that supply public access equipment to post signs reminding users about the need to comply with copyright law. One further step to consider, if the equipment is in a secure area or locked cabinet that requires users to get a key from library staff, is for a staff person to have the user sign a statement assuming full responsibility for complying with copyright law. Obviously, if the library is producing products, it can make certain that compliance occurs. A question arises about accepting multimedia courseware from instructors without some type of protection for the library in the event the developer failed to get the required permission(s).

Licensing agreements are a relatively recent issue for libraries and collection development staff. Initially, library staff paid little attention to such agreements. Acquisition staff signed the agreements and returned them without fully understanding what they were signing.

Financial and technical considerations are what staff talk about most after they address other concerns. In times of tight budgets, which seem to be the norm, budgeting for high-priced electronic materials represents a challenge. Balancing quality, quantity and cost is the fundamental task of collection development staff. The fact that electronic materials tend to be expensive for single-user agreements and even more expensive for multiple-user agreements, makes it even more difficult to answer the question: how much benefit to how many users? Does enhanced searching capability justify the purchase? What must be given up in other areas? Shifting resources from monographs, to serials, to electronics is a finite game for most libraries and information centers. Sometimes, additional funding is available for electronic materials, particularly when funding bodies view it as enhancing the image of the parent institution. As the glamour of electronic material delivered to individual workstations fades, so does the additional funding. Sometimes, the trade off involves canceling low-use serials to gain enough money to cover the DDS costs for acquiring both the occasionally needed article from the canceled titles and a few articles from titles never held.

The question of formats is also a question of technology and money. Realistically, additional funding will come from direct and indirect charges paid by end users. These charges will, at best, cover only the cost of the information, not the support, training, staffing, equipment and maintenance costs, thus creating an overall net cash drain and cost shift from other areas—often print collection funds. Because electronic information access offers the potential of end users having full control of their searches and acquisition of data, cost containment will likely become an important consideration.

For example, initial costs will vary depending on how the organization decides to handle its connections with electronic services, such as the Internet. There are three basic options for handling such service: terminal access, SLIP or PPP and leased line. Terminal access employs someone else's host computer. This approach eliminates host computer overhead and operating costs. Institutional costs are a registration fee, a monthly access charge and hourly connect charges. (This approach is similar to the one employed by Prodigy, America Online, Compu Serve and other online services).

A major disadvantage of this option is that the hourly connect charges are unknown until the monthly bill arrives. It is not uncommon for active users employing this option to accumulate monthly charges in excess of $700. Unsophisticated searchers, or experienced searchers without software that permits them to do some of the search formulation offline, can run up large bills. If users do not have to pay the costs, they have little incentive to improve their searching methods or to limit use time. Employing the serial line Internet protocol (SLIP) or point-to-point protocol (PPP) option provides more control over the connect costs. Many suppliers of these services charge an annual fee for unlimited connect time and no hourly charges. The disadvantage is that the annual fee will vary depending on the number of users. Additional charges are for local host capability for TCP/IP (transmission control protocol/Internet Protocol) as well as the technical expertise to manage the host. Though this capability and expertise probably exist in most academic and other large organizations, a question may arise as to whether the people with the capability have the time and willingness to take on the extra work.

Collection Development and the Web

As most librarians are aware, Web materials are a mixed bag ranging from solid, scholarly material to junk. Developing an appropriate collection of Websites brings to mind, at least for older librarians, the efforts to create and maintain the "vertical file pamphlet" collection. Print vertical files contained free or inexpensive items, but were labor-intensive to maintain. Web-site collections are the same in those two regards. The difference is in usage vertical files seldom did and certainly now do not receive as much use as one would like. Because the Web is popular with the public, usage is higher and if the library provides network access to its electronic material, the material is probably available 24 hours a day, which will further increase use.

In a presentation at the 1997 Internet Librarian conference in Monterey, California, Hope Tillman suggested that the Web and print-world publishing are much the same in the range of material (<http:www.tiac.net/ users/

hope/findqual.html>). That is, both range from vanity pieces to the very scholarly. She made the point that personal home pages are a form of vanity publishing. Experienced collection development officers know that not all self-publishing is poor quality or without value. What is different is that self-publishing does not go through the "vetting" process that takes place with other forms of publishing. The vetting/review process of print publishing serves the very useful purpose of imparting at least some degree of quality assurance. Websites that one knows are equally vetted are the equivalent of the scholarly print publications. The key is that one "knows" this to be the case. The Web also allows people to make any type of representations about themselves and what they are putting on the Web.

The essentials of Website evaluation are the same as for print. The challenge arises from the fact that there are fewer quick clues to quality in the Web environment. Where Web and print publishing differ is in the amount of promotional/advertising material. Not that print is not also filled with similar material, but it can be much more difficult to determine whether Web data is actually promotional and advertising material. It is not too difficult to determine when something on television or a printed page is advertising, even the so-called television "infomercials". With self-published material on the Web, it is often hard to tell where information ends and advertising begins.

Thus, determining Web quality is a bit more challenging than with printed material. Determining quality is challenging for several reasons. First, there is the changing nature of Web material. What was good yesterday may be poor or bad today and *vice versa*. This requires one to look for a last revised, modified, updated statement that one finds on quality Websites ... as well as some not-so-good sites. At least one gets some sense of the age of the material; naturally, a current date does not necessarily guarantee that the material was in fact modified. Another factor making evaluation more challenging is lack of knowledge about the "publisher". With a book from a commercial or university press, selectors have a history of quality of prior publications to draw upon. The best indicator one has for Websites is information contained in the URL.

If it implies it is from an academic institution, ".edu", one has a little stronger sense the material is at least not promotional or advertising. Though most educational institutions do not closely monitor the content of pages posted, most do have rules against using the institutional resources in a manner that would harm the institutional image, as well as forbidding individuals from engaging in commercial activity.

Electronic materials will be an ever-growing part of collections and user expectations.

Balancing these various elements demands constant adjustments in how libraries think about services and the most cost-effective approach. One must keep up-to-date on changing technology, changing players in the marketplace and user needs and wants. Further, libraries must do what they can to maintain a balance between producers' economic interests and rights and users' rights to fair use. It will be an ongoing challenge to libraries and information centers for years to come. By engaging in careful planning (including the preparation of an electronic collection policy), employing sound selection criteria and monitoring the use of the resources, libraries will meet the challenge.

REFERENCES

Antelmon, K. and D. Lagenberg. "Collection Development in the Electronic Library". *Association for Computing Machinery SIGUCCS* 21 (1993): 50-56.

Davis, T. L. "The Evolution of Selection Activities for Electronic Resources". *Library Trends* 45 (Winter 1997): 391-404.

Demas, S., P. McDonald and G. Lawrence. "The Internet and Collection Development: Mainstreaming Selection of Internet Resources". *Library Resources Technical Services* 39, no. 3 (July 1995): 275-90.

Eaton, E. K. "Information Management Systems Planning: A Process for Health Sciences Libraries and Institutions". In *Advances in Librarianship,* vol. 15. Edited by I. Godden, 13 1-57. New York: Academic Press, 1994.

Fedunok, S. "Hammurabi and the Electronic Age: Documenting Electronic Collection Decisions". *RQ* 36 (Fall 1996): 86-90

Flanagan, M. "Database Licensing: A Future View". *Computers in Libraries* 13 (January 1993): 21-22.

Gammon, J. A. "EDI and Acquisitions". *Library Acquisitions: Practice and Theory* 18 (Spring 1994): 113-23.

Hastings, S. K. "Selection and Evaluation of Networked Resources". *Acquisitions Librarian* 20 (1998): 109-22.

Hunter, K. "National Site License Model". *Serials Review* 18, nos. 1/2(1992): 71-72.

Johnson, P. and B. MacEwan, eds. *Collection Management and Development: Issues in an Electronic Era.* Chicago: American Library Association, 1994.

Martin, K. F. and R. F. Rose. "Managing the CD-ROM Collection Development Process: Issues and Alternatives". *Collection Management* 21, no. 2 (1996): 77-101.

Pack, T. "Electronic Books: A New Spin on the Great American Novel". *CD-ROM Professional* 7 (March 1994): 54-56.

Sasse, M. L. and B. J. Winkler. "Electronic Journals: A Formidable Challenge for Libraries". In *Advances in Librarianship,* vol. 17. Edited by I. Godden, 149-73. New York: Academic Press, 1993.

Sutherland, L. "Copyright and Licensing in the Electronic Environment". *Serials Librarian* 23, nos. 3/4 (1993): 143-47.

Woodward, H. M. "Impact of Electronic Information on Serials Collection Management". *IFLA Journal* 20, no. 1 (1994): 35-45.

Valauskas, E. J. "Reading and Computers: Paper-Based or Digital Text: What Is Best?" *Computers in Libraries* 14 (January 1994): 44-47.

Zarnosky, M. "Knowledge Served on a Silver Platter: Planning and Paying for CDROMs". *RQ* 32 (Fall 1992): 75-84.

9

Deselection Issues in Digital Library

We know vast space, staff and money is required to maintain the huge collections of books in libraries. Most of the big libraries face this problem as to store the new titles has become very difficult. Digitization is one solution to this problem.

In the present chapter we will elucidate the issue of 'deselection' or retirement of the books from the libraries.

It should be no surprise to read that libraries have had, and continue to have, serious problems with collection storage space. If one cannot get money for collections or staff, one can imagine how difficult it is to secure funding for additional space for either users or collections. The result is many libraries have had to engage one or more deselection projects in the recent past. Even if there has been a decline in the number of items acquired, there has been a steady growth of the collections; it has just been slower than in the past. "Selection in reverse" is one way to think about weeding or collection control.

Deselection, or weeding, is something most librarians thought about but seldom did in the past. However, this process is as important as the other steps in collection development. Without an ongoing weeding program, a collection can quickly age and become difficult to use. Although the major function of a library is to acquire, store, and make available knowledge resources, it is obvious that no library can acquire and store the world's total production of knowledge resources.

Some of the world's largest libraries like the Library of Congress, the British Library, Bibliotheque Nationale, and others do acquire most important items. Nevertheless, even these giants of the library world cannot do it all. Eventually, when they reach the limit of their growth, they confront, as the smallest library does, three alternatives: (1) acquire new physical facilities, (2) divide the collection (which also requires space), or (3) weed the collection. Only with new, adequate storage area can a librarian avoid selecting items for relocation. The need to find space for collections is a problem almost as old as libraries themselves. One of the earliest references to the problem in the United States was a letter from Thomas Hollis to Harvard College's Board of Governors in 1725. He wrote, "If you want more room for modern books, it is easy to remove the less useful into a more remote place, but do not sell them as they are devoted."

H. F. McGraw defined weeding (called stock relegation in the United Kingdom) as "the practice of discarding or transferring to storage excess copies, rarely used books, and materials no longer of use." He defined *purging* as "officially withdrawing a volume (all entries made for a particular book have been removed from library records) from a library collection because it is unfit for further use or is no longer needed." Libraries seldom destroy purged items. Disposal takes several forms: gifts and exchange programs, Friends of the Library book sales, or sale to an out-of-print dealer for credit against future purchases. Occasionally, the material goes into a recycling program.

The result is that a patron who may later request a purged item will have to use interlibrary loan to secure a copy.

In contrast storing retains the item at a second level of access. Second-level access normally is not open to the client and is frequently some distance from the library. Most second-level access storage systems house the materials as compactly as possible to maximize storage capacity. Corn-pact shelving for low-use material is coming into widespread use as libraries attempt to gain maximum storage from existing square footage. Generally, a staff member retrieves the desired item from the storage facility for the user.

It is pertinent to note before implementing a deselection program, the collection development staff should review deselection policies and goals. This review should include an analysis of the present staffing situation, consideration of alternative approaches, the feasibility of a weeding program in terms of other library operations, user interest and cooperation in such a project, types of materials collected, and cost. Some of the data for the program should come from collection evaluation projects that the selection officers and others undertake on a regular basis.

An active (i.e., ongoing) deselection program should be part of the library's collection development policy.

In fact, selection and weeding are similar activities: first, they are both necessary parts of an effective collection development program; and second, both require the same type of decision-making rules. The same factors that lead to the decision to add an item lead to a later decision to remove the item. Book selection policy should determine deselection activities. Collection policies, if properly prepared, help reduce space problems by controlling growth.

Nevertheless, the time eventually comes when collection space no longer accommodates additional material.

When this happens, some hard, costly decisions confront the library: build a new building, split the collection and use remote storage, or reduce the collection size. All three alternatives involve time-consuming and expensive processes. A policy of continuous deselection is more effective in the long run. Lazy librarians, like lazy gardeners, will find that the weeding problem only gets larger the longer they wait to do the job.

Deselection by Type of Library

Since different types of libraries have significantly different clientele and goals, they approach deselection from different points of view. Although the basic problems, issues, and methods of deselection apply to all libraries, variations occur in how they select the weeds and what they do with the weeds after pulling them.

1. Public Libraries: Public libraries may be viewed as supplying materials that meet the current needs and interests of a diverse community of users. In the public library, user demand is the important factor influencing selection and deselection. Therefore, materials no longer of interest or use to the public are candidates for storage or disposal. Usually, only large municipal public libraries consider storage, because their collections include research materials. As for discarding, a public library rule of thumb is that collections should completely turn over once every 10 years. Actual practice probably falls far short of that goal.

Storage, when undertaken, usually involves separating little-used books from the high-use working collection and discarding duplicates, worn-out volumes, and obsolete material. Some people claim that a collection containing many items of little interest is less useful, because high-demand items are not readily visible or accessible. Costs involved in maintaining a large collection are also a consideration.

Certainly there are differences due to size. Small and branch public libraries generally focus on high-demand materials, with little or no expectation that they will have preservation responsibilities. (An exception would be in the area of local history, where the library may be the only place one might expect to find such material.) Large public libraries have different responsibilities that often include housing and maintaining research collections. Thus they have to consider a wider range of issues, more like those confronting academic libraries, when undertaking a deselection program.

Sometimes a deselection project can have unexpected results; an example was the Free Library of Philadelphia. When the Philadelphia City Controller's office conducted its review of the library, it concluded that the library was in violation of the city charter by "destroying hundreds of thousands of books." Although the report acknowledged that weeding was a generally accepted practice in libraries, it also stated that "this practice had gone awry." At issue was the library's failure to try to find takers for the worn books it had withdrawn.

2. Special Libraries: "Special libraries" encompasses such a range of libraries as to make the category almost meaningless. Nevertheless, special libraries have to exercise the most stringent deselection programs, because of strict limits on collection size, usually the result of fixed amounts of storage space.

Paula Strain examined the problem of periodical storage

and cost of industrial floor space and found, not surprisingly, that the cost is so high that libraries must make efficient use of each square foot. The special library must operate with the businessperson's eye toward economy and efficiency.

Also, the collections of such libraries usually consist of technical material, much of it serial in character and often with a rapid and regular rate of obsolescence, at least for the local users. The major concern of special libraries is meeting the current needs of clients. In such a situation, deselection is easier because of comparatively straightforward and predictable use patterns, the small size and homogeneous nature of the clientele, and the relatively narrow service goals for the library. Deselection takes place with little hesitation because costs and space are prime considerations. Many of the bibliometric measures described in chapter 6 can be valuable in establishing deselection programs in special libraries.

3. Academic Libraries: Traditionally, the purposes of the academic research library have been to select, acquire, organize, preserve (this has had special emphasis), and make available the full record of human knowledge. Collection development officers in these institutions seldom view demand as a valid measure of an item's worth. Potential or long-term research value takes highest priority. This being said, why are deselection programs part of academic library collection development? The role of the college and university library is evolving. Whenever librarians discuss the changing role, they cite the information explosion as one cause. It is clear to most collection development staffs that it is futile to expect any one institution to locate and acquire all of the printed matter that comes into existence. Nor can they organize it, house it, or make it readily accessible to their public. No one person can manage to absorb all the relevant material that would be available, even if libraries could collect and preserve everything.

4. School Media Centers: School libraries and media centers employ highly structured collection development practices. In most schools and school districts, the media center expends its funds with the advice of a committee consisting of teachers, administrators, librarians, and, occasionally, parents. The need to coordinate collection development with curriculum needs is imperative. Typically, media centers lack substantial floor space for collections. Thus, when there is a major shift in the curriculum (new areas added and old ones dropped), the library must remove most of the old material. To some degree, the media centers deselection problems are fewer because there usually are other community libraries or a school district central media center that serve as backup resources.

Why Deselection?

It is pertinent to note that four reasons for implementing a deselection program appear regularly in the literature:

1) to save space
2) to improve access
3) to save money
4) to make room for new materials.

If the volume of literature on the subject reflected the degree to which libraries practiced deselection, there would be no need for conferences and workshops on the subject. Librarians spend more time writing about deselection than they do implementing the concepts. In part, this is because theory and the real world do not coincide. Often, from a realistic point of view, no other solution to space problems suggests itself except thinning the collection. When existing space fills up, and there is no additional collection space, the staff must do something.

Do theory and practice concerning space-saving coincide? Definitely! Compact storage systems save space. The conventional rule of thumb allows 15 volumes per square foot (500,000 volumes would require more than 33,000 square feet). A compact shelving system using a sliding shelf arrangement can store 500,000 volumes in slightly more than 14,000 square feet (an average of about 35 volumes per square foot)—a savings of more than 50 percent. Using a rail system of moving ranges, such as Space Saver, some libraries achieve savings of more than 80 percent. Less than 7,000 square feet can be used to house 500,000 volumes. The compact system recently installed at Loyola Marymount University will store 92,000 volumes in the same area that contained 24,000 volumes on conventional shelving.

Obviously, one pays a price for saving space, such as the extra cost of the compact system. However, Ralph Ellsworth, in *Economics of Book Storage in College and Research Libraries*, noted that conventional systems are also very expensive. Although his 1969 cost figures have not been updated, the relationships still hold: conventional shelving costs $1.31 per volume; sliding shelves, $1.24; and a moving range system, $0.91. Thus, one can lower the unit cost for stored items by using a compact storage system. However, he cost cited covers only the building and shelving; one must also consider several ether cost factors.

Archival libraries provide service, so our discussion naturally includes them, as they, too, eventually run out of space. However, service and size frequently do not go together. Anyone who has used a major research library knows that it takes time and effort to locate desired items.

Often, such a library is the only location for certain materials, which is clearly an important service. However, few clients claim that such libraries are easy or convenient to use. Most people still like everything to be convenient and easy to use. Thus, it is possible for a smaller, well-weeded collection to provide better service than a larger collection—as long as the smaller collection contains popular items.

Does deselection improve access? Here theory and practice start diverging. Some staff members and customers give enthusiastically positive answers. Others give equally definite negative responses. For those who require quick, easy access to high-use, current materials, the thoughtfully maintained collection becomes the ideal. However, for older, seldom-used materials housed in a remote storage facility, it may take some time to determine whether the library even owns the item, in addition to the time needed to retrieve it. Thus, the answer to the question of whether weeding improves access is sometimes yes, sometimes no. Finally, does weeding save money? Here the answer is probably no. Theory and reality are far apart at this point. As indicated, the cost per volume stored is usually lower using a compact storage system. However, one should consider several other important costs. For example, it is possible to quickly reduce the size of a collection by some arbitrary figure (5,000 volumes) or percentage (20 percent). One method of weeding in a public library would be to withdraw all books published before 1920 that have not circulated in the past five years. Just withdrawing the items from the shelves does not, however, complete the process. Staff must also change all the public and internal records to reflect the new status of the withdrawn books.

Though online catalogs and databases allow rapid record updating, there are still labor costs to consider.

Besides the cost of record modification, one must consider:

1. the cost of deciding which items to remove;
2. the cost of collecting and transporting them to their new location; and
3. the cost of retrieving items when needed.

Even if the storage system is less expensive per volume than conventional stacks, these hidden costs can quickly overtake the apparent savings.

Another cost, often overlooked, is the cost to customers. Delayed access to desired materials carries a user cost, if nothing more than negative public relations. Almost every customer wants items now, not in a few hours, much less days. In a research and development environment, retrieval delays may cost researchers valuable time and, perhaps, cost the organization money. Though difficult to determine or measure accurately, customer cost should be taken into account when evaluating the costs of deselection.

Limitations of Deselection

First a story of questionable veracity, but highlighting the major deselection barrier, concerns a collection development teacher. The teacher insisted that there was only one possible test to determine a person's suitability for becoming a collection development officer. Candidates would visit a doctor's office, where office staff would immediately take the candidate's blood pressure. The doctor would then hand the candidate a new book and tell the person to rip out one page and throw the book in a wastebasket. If the candidate's blood pressure rose above the initial reading, he or she would fail the test. True or not, the story does emphasize one of the most significant barriers to deselection-the psychological one. Parents and teachers teach most of us to treat books and magazines with respect. In fact, we learn a great respect for anything printed. The idea of tearing pages or otherwise damaging a book goes against all we have learned. The problem is that we are again confusing the information contained in a package with the packaging. Some material becomes dated and must go, or people will act on incorrect information (prime examples are a loose-leaf service with superseding pages or dated medical or legal information). Travel directories and telephone books are other examples of materials that should go. Long-term value of other materials is less clear, and it is easy to find reasons to save them. In essence, our childhood training adds to the difficulties in removing items from a collection. If the library's goal is to purge rather than store the item, the problem is even bigger.

No matter how long the candidate for storage or removal has remained unused, a collection development officer's reaction is, "someone will need it tomorrow." Also, an unused book or audiovisual raises two questions: "Why wasn't it used?" and "Why did the library buy it?" Like anyone else, collection officers are reluctant to admit to mistakes. The possibility of erroneously discarding some important items always exists. But to use fear of making a mistake as the reason for not engaging in deselection is inexcusable.

Another barrier, which is political as well as psychological, is created by patrons and governing boards. An academic library staff may feel that it needs to institute a weeding and storage program, but fails to do so because of faculty opposition. If experience is any indication, one can count on everyone being in favor of removing the dead wood-but not in their areas of interest.

Sometimes, librarians never suggest deselection because they assume that there will be opposition from faculty, staff, general users, board members, or others. Naturally, there will be opposition. However, if no one raises the issue, there is no chance of gaining customer support. The possibility also exists that the assumed opposition will never materialize and that customers from whom one least expects help turn out to be strong supporters. Fear of possible political consequences has kept libraries from proposing a deselection program.

Related to the political barrier is the problem of size and prestige. Many librarians, library boards, and customers rate libraries by size: the bigger the better. This brings us back to the epigraph of this book: "No library of a million volumes can be all BAD!" Quantity does not ensure quality. Collecting everything and throwing away nothing is much easier than selecting and deselecting with care.

Librarians risk no political opposition, their prestige remains high, and only the taxpayers and customers pay the price of maintaining everything the library ever acquired. Practical barriers to deselection also exist. Time can be a practical as well as a psychological barrier. The processes of identifying suitable deselec-tion criteria, developing a useful program, and selling that program require significant amounts of time. Beyond those steps, time is required for staff training, as is time to identify and pull the candidate items, to change the records, and, finally, to dispose of the weeds.

With a small library staff, it is difficult to mount a major deselection project because there are too many things to do with too few people. Starting a program is, inevitably, a major project for any size library. After completing the first project, the library should establish an ongoing deselection procedure and incorporate it into the normal workflow.

The ideal approach to a major project is to seek special funds and temporary staff to support the work. Occasionally, libraries encounter legal barriers. Although not common problems, when they do arise, they are time-consuming. The problem arises in publicly supported libraries where regulations may govern the disposal of any material purchased with public funds. In some cases, the library must sell the material, even if only to a pulp dealer. Any disposal that gives even a hint of government book-burning will cause public relations problems; this stems from general attitudes toward printed materials. The library should do all it legally can to avoid any such appearance.

Criteria

Remember! Deselection is not an overnight process, and it is not a function that one performs in isolation from other collection development activities. Persons involved in deselection must consider all library purposes and activities. Some of the most important issues are library goals, the availability of acquisition funds for new titles, the relationship of a particular book to others on that subject, the degree to which the library functions as an archive, and potential future usefulness of an item. Only when one considers all the factors can one develop a successful deselection program. After the staff recognizes the need for a deselection project, several lists of criteria can help in the deselection process.

H.F. McGraw developed the following fairly comprehensive list:

(a) duplicates

(b) unsolicited and unwanted gifts

(c) obsolete books, especially science

(d) superseded editions

(e) books that are infested, dirty, shabby, worn out, juvenile (which wear out quickly), and so forth

(f) books with small print, brittle paper, and missing pages

(g) unused, unneeded volumes of sets

(h) periodicals with no indexes.

The mere fact that a book is a duplicate or worn out does not necessarily mean that one should discard it. Past use of the item should be the deciding factor. Also, consider whether it will be possible to find a replacement copy. The books and articles cited earlier provide additional criteria.

Three broad categories of deselection criteria exist, at least in the literature: physical condition, qualitative worth, and quantitative worth. Physical condition, for most researchers, is not an effective criterion. In most cases, poor physical condition results from overuse rather than nonuse. Thus, one replaces or repairs books in poor physical condition. Consequently, if the library employs physical condition as a criterion, it will identify only a few items, unless brittle paper is part of the assessment process.

Any group assessment will be slow. Researchers have shown that a library can achieve almost the same outcome it would from specialists' reviewing the material by using an objective measure, such as past circulation or use data, if one wishes to predict future use. Also, the deselection process is faster and cheaper when past-use data are available.

C.A. Seymour summed up the issues regarding deselection as follows:

When the usefulness and/or popularity f a book has

been questioned, the librarian, if the policy of the library permits discarding, must decide:

(a) If the financial and physical resources are present or available to provide continuing as well as immediate housing and maintenance of the book;

(b) If the book can be procured, within an acceptably short time, from another library at a cost similar to, or lower than, the cost of housing and maintenance within the library;

(c) If allowing the book to remain in the collection would produce a negative value.

The problems that plague monograph weeding also apply to serials. A major difference, however, is that journals are not homogeneous in content. Another difference is that the amount of space required to house serial publications is greater than that required to house monographs. Thus, cost is often the determining factor in weeding.

No doubt, one should not forget the customer. Considering the benefits and disadvantages, in terms of customer service, that result from an active deselection program is a step in the process. Based on personal research projects, the percentage of librarians who think that a customer should be able to decide which materials to use out of all possible materials available (that is, no deselection) is much smaller than the percentage of librarians who strongly believe that a no-weeding policy is detrimental to the patron. Even academic faculty members lack complete familiarity with all the materials in their own subject fields; faced with a million volumes or more in a collection, how can we expect a student to choose the materials most helpful to his or her research without some assistance?

Large libraries, particularly research libraries, deselect for storage rather than for discarding. These are two different processes. Often, criteria useful in making discard decisions do not apply to storage decisions. It is important to recognize that the primary objective of these two different forms of treatment is not necessarily to reduce the total amount of money spent for library purposes. Instead, the primary objective is to maximize, by employing economical storage facilities, the amount of research material available to the patron. The two main considerations for a storage program are: (1) What selection criteria are most cost-effective? and (2) How will the library store the items?

A Yale University Library project, the Selective Book Retirement Program, has value for today's deselection project planners. The project funding came from the Council on Library Resources, with the expectation that the results would be useful to other libraries. Project staff were to determine how best to cope with the problem of limited shelf space while continuing to build quality research collections and provide good service. The council outlined the following objectives for Yale in Yale's Selective Book Retirement Program:

a. To expedite the Yale University Library's Selective Book Retirement Program (from 20,000 to 60,000 volumes per year) and to extend it to other libraries on the campus;

b. To study (in collaboration with the faculty) the bases of selection for retirement for various subjects and forms of material;

c. To study the effects of the Program on library use and research by faculty, graduate and undergraduate students;

d. To ascertain what arrangements may compensate for the loss of immediate access caused by the program;

e. To explore the possible effectiveness of the Program toward stabilizing the size of the immediate-access collection;

f. To publish for the use of other libraries the policies, procedures, and results thus discovered.

According to the report, the project staff fulfilled all the objectives but "d."

The Yale staff based their decisions about which books to move to storage on several factors :

1. A study of books on the shelves.
2. Value of a title as subject matter.
3. A volume's importance historically in the field.
4. Availability of other editions.
5. Availability of other materials on the subject.
6. Use of a volume.
7. Physical condition

Obviously, the selection process depended upon the subjective judgment of individual librarians, some of whom were subject bibliography specialists. The librarians determined that general policies regarding weeding were easier to formulate than those that applied to specific fields; that it was easier to recommend weeding of specific titles than groups or kinds of books in specific fields; and that unanticipated mechanical problems greatly affected weeding procedures. These last problems included:

1. Lack of regularity in weeding (i.e., finding an

adequate number of faculty and staff members and the time to keep the process going satisfactorily).

2. Diminishing returns over the long period (i.e., the longer the program existed, the more difficult the weeding process became

3. The "Ever-Normal-Granary" theory (one of the purposes of the selective retirement program was to discover whether a library can control the growth of its collection by annually removing from the stacks the same number of volumes it adds). It was discovered that for the theory to be practical, either fragmentation into department libraries must occur, or the library administration must be willing to manage its collection and facilities solely on the principle of stabilization-neither of which Yale was willing to do.

4. Disagreement among weeders (i.e., the narrower viewpoint of faculty because of subject specialty versus the broader viewpoint of the librarian).

Another unforeseen problem was a general feeling of discontent among faculty members and students. Neither group really understood the storage problem, and both objected to any change. Students particularly disliked the fact that they could not browse in the storage area.

Fussler and Simon reported some interesting ideas and statistical findings concerning the use factor in selective weeding of books for storage. Although they recognized that frequency of circulation or use of books is not always an accurate measure of the importance of books in large research libraries, Fussler and Simon hoped to determine whether some statistical method could identify low-use books in research library collections. One of their goals was to sort the collection into high- and low-use materials.

High-use items would remain in the local collection, and low-use items would go to a remote storage facility. They found that use and circulation data was effective for the first cut, that is, to identify potential materials. The final judgment of what to send to storage or discard remained with the collection development staff and other interested persons.

Blindly following use data can create more problems than it solves. The authors concluded that past use of an item was the best predictor of future use. Given the nature of a large research library, they thought a 15- to 20-year study period provided the best results, but a 5-year period provided adequate data.

Fussler and Simon's study is valuable because it outlines the factors that affect the validity of comparing criteria for removing books for storage, and because of their findings concerning the advantages of libraries devising similar rules.

These factors are helpful reminders to any library considering a deselection program:

1. Differences among libraries in composition of the collection in specific subject areas.
2. Differences in size of collections.
3. Differences in size of university populations.
4. Differences in nature of university populations.
5. Differences in kind of record-of-past-use.

In addition to factors that affect comparisons, Fussler

and Simon's findings indicate that their methods would produce similar percentages of use in libraries regardless of type, clientele, and collection size. They concluded that scholars at various institutions have similar reading interests.

Finally, they identified three practical alternatives for selecting books for storage:

1. Judgment of one or a few expert selectors in a field.
2. An examination of past use of a book and/or its objective characteristics.
3. A combination of these two approaches.

Obviously, of these alternatives, they concluded that an objective system (that is, a statistical measure) ranks books more accurately in terms of probable value than does the subjective judgment of a single scholar in the field. They did recommend, however, that subject specialists and faculty review the candidate books identified using objective means before moving the books to remote storage. Richard Trueswell quantitatively measured the relationship between the last circulation date of a book and user circulation requirements, and their effect on weeding. He hoped to determine a quantitative method of maintaining a library's holdings at a reasonable level while providing satisfactory service to the user.

Trueswell's basic assumption was that the last circulation date of a book is an indication of the book's value. He determined the cumulative distribution of the previous circulation data, which he assumed represented the typical circulation of a given library. Next, he determined the 99th percentile, which he used as the cutoff point for stack thinning. By multiplying the previous monthly circulation figures and the distribution for each month after establishing the 99th percentile, he was able to calculate the expected size of the main collection. In applying this method to a sample from the Deering Library at North-western University, Trueswell predicted that a library could satisfy 99 percent of its circulation requirements with just 40 percent of its present holdings. That is, the library could move 60 percent of its collections to storage without significantly affecting the majority of users.

Trueswell did admit that many of his basic assumptions were questionable and that future research would yield more reliable data. Additional research, including that by Trueswell, supported his initial results.

It is remarkable that another study of note is Aridamen Jain's *Report on a Statistical Study of Book Use*. This quantitative study of book use is based on extremely different assumptions from the two studies described previously. Though his statistical manipulations may completely baffle a nonstatistician, the theory behind Jain's method of measuring book use is easy to understand. The purpose of his study was to examine mathematical models and statistical techniques for determining the dependence of circulation rate on a book's age and on certain other characteristics. He hoped to indicate that the age of a book is the most significant variable both in predicting rates of monograph usage and in deciding which books to transfer to storage. He reviewed other studies concerned with determining whether the frequency with which groups of books with defined characteristics were likely to show use in a research library when identified through statistical methods.

He hoped to establish, through comparative methods, that the probability of a book not being used is an efficient method of predicting use by taking into account the age of the book. Jain's model seems to be particularly valuable in deselection projects, for two reasons. One is that, contrary to the total library collection sampling method used by Fussler and Simon, Jain, like Trueswell, derived his data from all of the books checked out for a specific time period (that is, without regard to the total library collection). Jain felt that this method was superior to that used by Fussler and Simon.

Although their method ensures the gathering of information on the same books over a longer time, Jain's method is much more conducive to a statistical design and data collection-missing data and lack of control are no longer problems. A second reason for this model's importance is that by using the specific time period sampling method, one can determine relative use of books within the library. With Fussler and Simon's method, this is not possible. Jain felt that the relative use concept was more efficient in studying the usage of books than the collection method.

Many other deselection studies exist, and they all generally agree that deselection based on past-use data provide the most cost-effective results. Although most of the studies were from academic libraries, Stanley Slote found that the method also worked in public libraries. Past use is a reasonable criterion if one is selecting for storage. However, the questions raised by the Urquharts indicate that librarians should go slowly in applying the past-use criterion when selecting items for purging. Researchers have investigated almost every conceivable combination of objective criteria at one time or another in hope of finding the best.

For example, they have examined language; date of publication; subject matter; frequency of citation; and listing in bibliographies, indexes, and abstracting services. Citation analysis and presence or absence of indexing or abstracting are most effective for serials and periodicals.

An interesting method for deselecting periodicals is to calculate a density-of-use value. The method requires establishing a unit of space occupied for each periodical title. Next, one determines the number of uses the title receives during a fixed time (perhaps one month). A ranking of the titles by use will produce one list, whereas a ranking by space occupied will probably result in a different list. Because one common objective of deselection programs is cost-effective use of existing collection space, calculating a ratio of space occupied to use (density of use) will help determine which periodicals to move to storage.

The preponderance of evidence points to the past-use criterion as the one most reliable for storage purposes. If the library has a circulation system that leaves a physical record of use in each book or in a database, one can easily collect the needed data. Today's automated circulation systems can provide detailed information about items, including frequency of circulation, class of borrower, use by class number, age of the item, language, and producer, as well as almost any other physical or intellectual content characteristic. Though circulation data is as sound a predictor of future use as one can find, it does rest upon several assumptions that staff must understand and accept. One assumption is that circulated use is proportional to in-house use. What that proportion is depends on local circumstances. A second assumption is that current use patterns are similar to past and future patterns. A third assumption is that statistically random samples provide an adequate base for determining use patterns. A known limitation of circulation data is that a few customers can have a major impact on circulation (otherwise known as the 80/20 rule). Failure to take in-house use into account in a deselection program dependent on use data as the main selection criterion will have skewed results. One factor to keep in mind is that the automated circulation systems now in use in many libraries will make it possible to collect valuable data for a project. With many systems, it is possible to collect data about in-house use by using a handheld reader and then downloading the data to the system.

In the past, in-house use data was particularly time-consuming to collect. The fourth edition of Slote's book has an excellent chapter on using computer data in a deselection project.

Some information professionals in a special library or information center environment find themselves in charge of the organization's paper files, or archive. Some academic libraries also have responsibility for the campus archive. Just as print and audiovisual collections eventually exceed the pace available, so do company files. When this happens, the equivalent of the library environment deselection process takes place. In the business setting, and when dealing with the organization's records, the term used for the process is retention.

A records retention program, developed by the person in charge of the files (who may be an information specialist, librarian, or records manager) is designed to meet several objectives:

1. assure protection of the organization's vital records
2. retain records of value or historical interest for the appropriate amount of time, meeting both legal and business needs for the records to be available
3. restrict storage equipment and floor space, in expensive areas, to active records

4. store inactive records in inexpensive storage facilities
5. release reusable material—audiotapes, magnetic tapes, or floppy disks-as quickly as possible
6. destroy records that have served their purpose and are no longer useful.

Records managers classify documents in several ways: as record or non-record, as active or inactive, and by value or use. A record is an official document of the organization; nonrecords are convenience copies. With a multiple-part order form, the original, or top copy, of the order is a record and all the other copies are nonrecords. Photocopies and carbon copies are almost always nonrecord items. *Active records* are those needed for current operating activities and consulted on a regular basis. The organization determines the cutoff period between active and inactive. Factors influencing the organization's decision include the amount and cost of available storage space and the cost of active space. Storage of inactive records normally occurs away from the mail facilities of the organization in special warehouses designed to store the inactive records of many organizations. Records managers determine value by the way people use the records. Typical categories of value are legal, operating, administrative, fiscal, research, and historical.

Appendices

APPENDIX - 1

COLLECTION DEVELOPMENT AT THE UNIVERSITY LIBRARY

Citation analyses have been applied to a number of library acquisition activities, yet the utility of these studies have often been questioned. Too often, such a study incorporates a "world wide" data set in a relatively broad discipline. This sort of approach may lack relevance to a specific University, its research specialities, and ultimately its library collection. In order to increase the relevance of this citation analysis to the local institution, sample size and subject focus were limited to the published works of a small group of the University's faculty. Relevance to the University was increased since the faculty at that very institution were studied.

The literature incorporated in their research constituted the entire sample rather than a small subset of a universal data set wherein many of the titles may never come near their campus. A byproduct of selecting a small group of local faculty is a very narrow subject focus, in this case statistics. Rather than scanning the mathematics literature and ranking those titles, only the titles directly applicable to statistics were considered and they were applicable to the University in question because they were cited by the faculty at the same institution. The results of this study are similar to other studies of physical science citation patterns, especially mathematics. For example, the study by Rousseau found that the average age of citations in the mathematics literature was much greater than those from other physical sciences, such as physics.

The average age of the material cited herein was 12.3 years. Most of the material cited was found in journals (46.7%) while monographs were cited 36.9% of the time. Most of the material cited by the faculty at Texas Tech University could be found in the University Library, 68.4% of the journals and 60.0% of the monographs.

Using the citation analysis as an evaluation tool, various journals and books could be considered for acquisition. While other tools may also be used for this purpose, such as Inter Library Loan statistics, citation analysis is viewed as a superior tool for examining the usefulness of a library collection to its patrons and as an important element of a collection development policy.

Literature Review

A brief survey of the literature illustrates the breadth and potential application of conducting a citation analysis. A substantial number of research papers, involving some aspect or application of bib metrics, have been published. The first five articles discussed here analyze the citation patterns of various physical sciences and three additional articles exemplify the usefulness of such studies.

Peters et. al. used the literature of Chemical Engineering to monitor scientific productivity or "research performance". They found bibliometric analysis to be a valuable tool. Their methodology seemed designed to reinforce rather than examine preconceived notions, however. They suggested that a citation analyses was not usefúl to the same extent in all sub-fields of chemical engineering since some scientists with "high reputations" turned out to be "bibliometrically invisible". Twenty-one "significant" journals of oceanography were examined by Garfield. Here too, a concern was raised over sub-fields within the discipline. For the purpose of this study, oceanography meant chemical and physical oceanography. Marine biology was excluded. Garfield's intent here was to prioritize journal titles worldwide using the citation patterns of titles from this "core" list.

The work by Spies reviewed fourteen "major" journals of exploration geophysics for "effectiveness". This paper presented a basic tenet of citation analysis as follows: the references that an author cites are a roughly valid indicator of influence, hence value, to his work. A measure of cost effectiveness was also incorporated into this study as subscription costs and citation rates were compared between commercial publications and those produced by professional societies.

Uzun et. al. studied the citation rates of 572 Turkish physics publications that appeared in the source journals listed in the Science Citation Index. This analysis was global in scope, as is commonly the case with citation studies. They examined impact factor, immediacy index, citation frequency, and the nationality of the publishing house. The question which these normal parameters and this normal scope raise for librarians is-"How is this relevant to the local collection for which I have a responsibility to build based upon the research and curriculum program ongoing at my institution"?

Finally, Rousseau presented a citation distribution of mathematics journals, wherein he proposes that a four-year impact factor would be more suited to mathematics than the more or less typical two-year impact factor used in

Science Citation Index. Once again, the question of relevancy presents itself.

Three additional sources were examined which addressed the practical application of bibliometrics. Bookstein sought to establish a foundational argument in favor of using citation patterns for collection development. Garfield also claimed that the frequency of journal citations could be used in collection development, even so as to select particular titles of local interest in order to address this issue of relevancy. The article by Swigger and Wilkes attempted to broaden the scope of factors used in collection development decisions to include professional judgment of librarians, faculty requests, and use studies. In actuality, this appears to be the most realistic method. They concluded that no one method is totally valid but that citation analyses offered the most reliable approach.

Methods

It is evident from this brief survey that citation studies have been conducted on a wide variety of disciplines for diverse reasons. The purpose of this section is to present a simple, practical, relevant tool to assist in the collection development process.

The first step was to identify a specific and workable sub-field of a discipline. As the library liaison to the Mathematics Department, I chose statistics, which consisted of seven faculty members. These individuals were chosen based on the list of faculty research interests provided by the Mathematics Department.

The second step was to search for the published works of each faculty member identified in step one within a suitable time frame. The current and previous years were chosen since they would reflect the most relevant research interests of this group of faculty. Additionally, some members of this group had recently requested that the Library subscribe to a new journal title which began publication by Gordon and Breach in 1991, Journal of Nonparametric Statistics. In order to incorporate this title into the present study and evaluate its suitability for addition to the collection, only recently published articles could be considered. Citations to this title would not be expected to appear in print before 1993 due to the time required for an article to be submitted, reviewed, revised, and appear in print: 18 months to two years.

The following sources were searched: Books in Print, INSPEC, World Cat, Uncover, Math Reviews, Statistical Theory and Methods Abstracts, and Zentralblatt fur Mathematik und Ihre Grenzgbiete. E-Math, via an Internet connection to the American Mathematical Association, was also used to search Math Reviews a second time.

The third step was to collect the articles found in step two, using InterLibrary Loan as necessary and to review the citation patterns. The entire article was needed, not just the list of references at the end of the article since the number of citations throughout the paper must be considered. Other items of interest may be revealed, as in this case, where the pattern of nonbibliographic citations added an unexpected dimension to this study.

The fourth step was to document the results.. Step five involved analyzing the results. Finally, the findings should be applied to collection development decisions such as purchasing previously unowned but heavily cited items.

Results/Application

Two citation patterns were identified, bibliographic and nonbibliographic citations. Both groups may be applied to the collection development process. Fourteen print journal articles were found to be published by the sample faculty in 1993 and the first half of 1994. No books and no electronic sources were identified.

The bibliographic citations were arbitrarily divided into two groups, those cited three or more times and those cited fewer than three times. Those cited more than three times constitute 72% of the citations in 31% of the titles. This group is, subsequently, of greater interest to collection development considerations. My goal is to provide at least 90% of the journals and monographs found in this group of 38 titles. The present composition is as follows:

Two journals would need to be added to reach my goal. Therefore, during the next round of discussions, given to this topic, I recommended that the following titles be added to the collection:

- Journal of Time Series analysis
- Stochastic Processes and Their Applications

The three monographs found in this top group, not owned by TTU, have been added to the collection, thereby the collection development decision to support this research by acquiring enough titles to bring library holdings up to 90% of the frequently cited titles was made and acted upon.

Overall, 394 citations were found in 122 titles, having the following composition: Additionally, five titles were never cited and eighteen citations referred to either an unclear title or no title at all in the references at the end of the paper.

Obviously, print journals provided the most research

support with monographs coming in a close second. The age of this material is also important, especially in light of the request to add a new journal subscription to the library holdings, Journal of Nonparametric Statistics. What support is there for such a request? The requested title began publication in 1991. The average age of the most heavily cited works (cited three or more times) is 11.2 years and over all of the titles, 12.3 years. This title would not be expected to contribute to the research of this faculty group for some time to come, based upon this citation analysis. In fact, this title was not cited once. Not one faculty member published a paper in this journal and not one ILL request has been made from this institution for this title during the past two years. Therefore, there is no objective substantiation for this purchase.

Various subjective factors must also be considered and it is interesting to consider the weight of subjective versus objective criteria in this process. Science and scientists strive for objectivity, yet science is done by scientists who are by their nature, subjective and not objective. The request for this title was made on the basis of the editorial board and the appearance of sample and refereed articles, no measurable qualities. In balancing the equation between art and science, in this case, art tipped the scale and the title was ordered.

The nonbibliographic citations provided an unexpected and useful resource for collection development. Each of the papers in this study referred to (cited) various sources but did not list those sources in a bibliography, hence I have labeled them "nonbibliographic citations". These titles may be found in a dictionary or encyclopedia of mathematics where they are described and placed in the context of the research literature of the field. A list of citations to the original work or works is often included in these Reference sources. The "title" as presented here, offers a topic of apparent research interest to this population of faculty. Books, journals, and other materials related to the most heavily cited topics should be considered for inclusion in the collection. Since a specific title must be matched to a particular topic, another "recommendation" for the title, such as a scholarly review, may be appropriate before a collection development decision is made.

The topics cited most frequently in these papers included Hermitian operators, Appel polynomials, Laplace transform, Euclidean space, Drichlet polynomials, Lebesgue measure, Hilbert space, and Taylor expansion. Entering these terms in WorldCat resulted in a variety of hits. I narrowed the list to recent titles, generally 1993 and 1994 to come up with a list of books relevant to the research interests of this group of faculty. Unfortunately, very few book reviews could be found to evaluate these titles. In some cases, we already had the title. Most, we did not own. I have placed orders for several titles, matching the topical interest of the nonbibliographic citations found in this study.

In conclusion, this study provided new and foundational data to characterize and measure the research activity of a local group of mathematicians. This data could contribute to a larger project where results could be compared with other disciplines, both closely and distantly related. The nonbibliographic citations added a new dimension to the citation analysis of the physical sciences which has not been previously described. Objective and substantive information was gathered to provide criteria for collection development decisions.

The relationship between research and teaching in the context of serial subscriptions is important though indirect.

Never the less, basic research supports teaching as a foundation supports a structure. Faculty may occasionally assign readings from their own published works for undergraduate use, yet the collection development decision to subscribe to a journal is more heavily influenced by its direct role in research rather than teaching.

APPENDIX 2

DIGITAL LIBRARIES IN JAPAN & EDUCATION

In Japan the emphasis today appears to be in getting content online, with the main emphasis on rare books and manuscripts, theses and journal articles. University-level educational research is and will be possible, because university libraries will be the repositories of this information. Until sharing across digital libraries is possible, it is not likely that there will even be such research across universities. In the United States the concept of sharing is agreed upon; in Japan, it does not seem to be.

In the United States, there is also a big recognition of the interplay between education and the digital library. That same recognition does not appear to be so prevalent in Japan. Digital libraries do not appear to be making an impact in K-12 education. The Ministry of Education (MIE) is providing resources so that every elementary and middle school will have 20 computers, and every high school will have 40 computers; but the MIE is reluctant to provide resources for communications (e.g., Internet connections). This means that it is very problematic that students will be able to go online and make use of the digital libraries.

In Japan, it is very prestigious and important for a student to be admitted into an important university, such as Tokyo University or Kyoto University. So a market exists for companies to prepare students to take university entrance exams, for which students' parents will spend a lot of money. There is no market for K-12 students while they are in K-12, however, which is one of the reasons that Nikkei, a company that is very heavily involved with digital information, is not interested in this student population.

At Keio University, there is the Humanities Media Interface Project (HUMI project), which was launched in Spring 1996 with the aim, among others, of digitizing major rare books and manuscripts. Western, Japanese and Chinese in the Keio collection, including the Keio Gutenberg Bible. The HUMI Project has been supported by the Ministry of Education, Science, Sports and Culture (*Monbusho*), the Information-Technology Promotion Agency (IPA), which is attached to the Ministry of International Trade and Industry, and Keio University. The library has a very large collection of rare books, including 8,000 Western rare books. The project managers seem to have a very progressive view of digitization of books, namely that, once digitized, the books can be examined or reassembled any way a person wants. The Keio Gutenberg Bible has played a very important role in the HUMI Project. The Bible was acquired not just for possession of an important article of Western cultural heritage, but because Keio University believes that modern research libraries should possess works significant enough to be digitized for the benefit of today's scholars. The university also wishes to promote the greater goal of preserving these treasures for posterity without further decay. For more discussions about the visit to Keio University, see the site report in Appendix C.

The HUMI Project is a clear indication that some very serious work is indeed occurring in Japan regarding education and digital libraries, and suggests that much more may indeed be occurring than we had the opportunity to observe directly. Prof. Naohito Okude (Keio University) sent this author some important observations about the digital library in education, in an e-mail message. Professor Okude's comments are paraphrased below, because not only are they somewhat visionary, but because they are also very optimistic about education using digital libraries:

Contrary to the general assumption that hypermedia obliterates the past, digital technology is radically reconfiguring our understanding of history. Being digital in a research library requires designing a post-Gutenbergian research model for the humanities. Digital technology forces us to recognize that texts are not higher than images. Computers rid us of the assumption that sensory messages are incompatible with reflection. Once digitized, fleeting images become available to anyone who "reads" them on a graphics computer. Imaging becomes a rich and fascinating mode for communicating ideas.

In order to conduct a professional image search within the humanities, serious training in visual proficiency is needed. The image search is an activity of focusing on cross-disciplinary problems in arts, graphics, film, video, media production and their different histories.

Learning has always been a people-to-people process. Digital library technology will promote a computer-mediated people-to-people learning process. This technology will have to expand from its traditional areas, such as information retrieval and distance learning, to the new frontier of information work application to assist distributed learning and the process of inquiring using a networked system.

Computer-human interface should be a central research agenda item for digital libraries. In addition to keyboards and mice, trackballs and joysticks, as well as gloves, helmets, glasses and body-suits, move an object on a computer screen. These multi-modal interfaces are not only immature in their development status, but they also are not intelligent. Future interfaces will be intelligent and will mediate communication between the researcher and the distributed computer network to make the latter more responsive to the former's wants and needs. New multi-modal intelligent interfaces will let the researcher span the continuum from passive reception of research data to active creation of new research results.

Virtual reality (VR) technology is most appropriate for representation as well as research. Bit-mapped graphics-based supercomputers can run high-speed graphics and track human movements. Immersion, interactivity, and information intensity are the three main characteristics of VR technology. In the next ten years we can expect a widespread and growing experience of VR in a variety of everyday educational and learning environments.

The real market for digital technology is not the "information market" but the "information work" market. The technologies for information work let a person or a computer program take in information, transform it, and send it out. Today's content creation technologies do not yet fulfill these functions.

When people and organizations all have computers, and all these computers are interconnected, they will sell and freely exchange information and information services. The digital libraries will then take the role of information managers in the age of the convergence of communication and computation, and new distribution technologies will emerge to link one digital library with other digital libraries, in order to effect digital data assistance. The role of the nineteenth-century library as the custodian of physically printed materials will remain but the digital libraries will also become distributed information managers of the links to other digital libraries. A grand distributed global digital library is the dream and the final goal of the digital libraries endeavor.

Each library will someday offer its collection in electronic form. To users, the collection of worldwide distributed libraries will look like one uniform library. To achieve interoperability of digital data at this level, enhancements of networking capabilities, interface design, and object-oriented databases are needed. Without this open architecture and deployment of distributed object-oriented technology, there is no future for the digital library to scholars and other people who want to use the libraries for their creative activities. Every library around the world should communicate with each other so as to contribute a consolidation of diverse human knowledge and experience.

Education and learning will be the huge market when the distributed digital libraries and the information work technologies are available to the content creators. Education and learning are lifelong pursuits. Within a few decades, people in Japan will come to the university at irregular times and will take more than four years to graduate. They will study for more years and will study more. This fragmented and discontinuous pattern is more of an expectation than the norm now, but students in the future will attend in broken times, and will often learn from more than one institution. This knowledge consumer market is the digital libraries' business domain.

Glossary

Aberrant copy - a copy of a book containing obvious printing and/or binding errors that are more serious than minor defects.

Aberrant date - in archives, a date that falls outside the chronological sequence of dates pertaining to the majority of the documents in the record unit described (Richard Pearce-Moses, *A Glossary of Archival and Records Terminology*, Society of American Archives).

absorption - the incorporation of one serial by another. The note *Absorbed:* followed by the title of the assimilated serial is added to the bibliographic record representing the assimilating publication, and the corresponding note *Absorbed by:* followed by the title of the assimilating serial is added to the record for the assimilated publication. The absorbed title usually assumes the title and numbering of the assimilating publication. Compare with merger.

Abstract - a brief set of statements that summarize, classifies, evaluates, or describes the important points of a text, particularly a journal article. An abstract is typically found on the first page of a scholarly article. Because an abstract summarizes an article, it is very useful for either browsing or keyword searching.

Annotation - an explanatory or critical note or commentary. Annotation is also the process of adding an explanatory or critical note or commentary to a text. Reference lists are often annotated with comments about what each resource covered and how useful it was.

Appendix - a group of supplementary material appended to a text. It is usually related to the material in the main part of the text but not so closely related to it that it should be put into the main text. Put background information and supporting facts in the appendices. An example of a file that should be put in an appendix is a file of detailed charts and graphs of recent research closely related to the paper's main topic.

Archive - a place in which historical documents and other records are preserved. Usually operated by large organizations, they may or may not be open to the public. The University of Toronto, for example has an archive that requires a five story building and contains several climate controlled vaults. A virtual archive is similar except the documents have no physical presence and seldom have historical value.

Author - an originator of a creative work, particularly a writer of a text. Searching by author can be an effective form of information gathering.

Bibiographic database is a computer based list of library resources. Typically each record contains the call number, author, title, publishing information, and other card catalog information.

Bibliography - a list of writings related to a specific subject, writings by a specific author, or writings used in producing a specific text.

Boolean logic - the algebraic system, developed by George

Boole that is applied to Boolean expressions that contain Boolean operators such as AND, OR, NOT AND, and XOR (exclusive OR). This binary algebraic system is used primarily in switching circuits and database searches. Boolean operators are not to be confused with proximity operators such as NEAR.

Browse - to inspect something casually, particularly to use an internet browser to casually inspect Web pages. This involves following links from page to page (also called surfing) rather than searching directly. The main difference between browsing and searching is that with browsing you have very little advance knowledge of what will be on the next page.

Call number - an identification marker used in libraries to categorize and locate books and other resources. Each resource is assigned a combination of letters and numbers which correspond with a location in the library. For example the call number for the Publication Manual of the American Psychological Association is BF76.7 .P83 2001.

Catalog (or catalogue) - a complete and systematically organized enumeration of items, particularly the complete enumeration of a libraries' resources on a set of paper cards (card catalog) or in an electronic database (bibliographic database).

Citation - the quoting or mentioning of a source. All works used in preparing a paper should be cited.

Citation search - a search, by name, of all references to an individual. Some databases have a specific citation search option, otherwise you use a full-text search. For an example of a database that has a specific citation search option go to the University of Michigan Library Database.

Community analysis - the analysis of a set of people. Such analyses enable librarians to know the needs of patrons and hopefully provide better services to them. In a city library district, the set of relevant people would be all those who live in the city or those people eligible to use the library. Analysis may also be restricted to a subset of eligible library users.

Controlled vocabulary - limiting searches to the exact subject headings contained in the Library of Congress. An example would be "History - Bibliography etc". Some indexes, like Wilson Indexes, have their own system of headings and hence their own controlled vocabulary.

Copyright - the legal right granted to a copyright holder for the exclusive sale, distribution or reproduction of a creative work. It is a form of intellectual property that prevents others from using a creative work without consent of the owner. For example, Thomas Mann holds the copyright on the book The Oxford Guide to Library Research.

Cross reference database - a collection of records that have one or more fields that reference other related records. These connections (for example between "marketing" and "promotion") make browsing very productive and allow related-items searches.

Descriptor - an index term used to identify a record in a database. It can consist of a word, phrase, or alphanumerical term. It can describe the content of the record or be an arbitrary code. When a descriptor is descriptive, it can be an effective search parameter.

Dissertation - a written treatise or thesis, usually lengthy, usually authored by a doctoral candidate, usually directed by a faculty advisor, and usually intended to advance the state of the art in a given discipline. There can be an oral component to the process, in which the dissertation must be defended in front of critical judges. Dissertation searches are valuable because of their currency.

Document delivery - the transfer of a database record, or other information resource, to the end user. It can involve direct internet or email transfers, CD delivery via mail, paper delivery via mail, or delivery via interlibrary loan.

Edition - a version of a published text, or all the instances of a published text issued at a given time. An example would be the 2nd edition (2001).

Entry - any record, or a field in a record, that has been included, or entered, into a database. An **entry word** is the headword in a dictionary, encyclopedia, or glossary.

Field - an element of a database record. It contains one type of information and has a unique address. All or most other records in the database have a similar field. An example is the field "name".

Free-text search - 1. is a simple word or character search, usually with very few Boolean, proximity, or scope limiting options. It is simple and fast. 2. a search in which all the entries are freed from their original format of presentation. Text that originated in a journal article looks much the same as text that originated in a glossary or chat room. 3. the deliberate limiting of the scope of the search parameters to include only records that are available free of charge.

Full text database - a collection of records containing

complete versions of the original source, rather than just bibliographies, abstracts, or abridgements. An example is JSTOR. A related concept is that of a full text search which searches only sources that are complete, and ignores those records that are mere abstracts or descriptors.

Interlibrary loan - when patrons of a library arrange for resources from other libraries to be sent to their library. This resource sharing system is being promoted by the International Federation of Library Associations.

Journal - a periodical publication that presents articles in a specific subject area. They are usually scholarly. An example is *The Journal of Marketing Research*.

Keyword searching - the searching of a database using a significant word from the title, abstract, or descriptor of a record as a point of reference to the article's overall content. This type of search is usually the best type to start with.

Literature search - A systematic and thorough search of all material, print or electronic, published on a given topic. This can include books, journals, newspapers, catalogs, encyclopedias, dictionaries, atlases, bibliographies, handbooks, manuals, indexes, yearbooks, gazetteers, directories, chronologies, almanacs, and guides.

Menu - a list of options from which a computer user can choose. This saves the user from having to memorize a set of commands. It also reduces the decision down to the basic information required (note the etymology from the French word minuet meaning small).

Monograph - a written document (i.e., graph) on a single subject (i.e., mono). It is usually scholarly in nature and of approximately book length. They are valuable information sources because of their depth in a limited subject area.

Online catalog - a record of the holdings of an institution (usually a library), or group of institutions, that can be found on the internet. An example is UCSD's "Roger".

Open sources software (OSS)- oss are software which is available free for use, run, distribute. It can not be used for commercial benefit.

Operators - symbols that represent operations. In computer science there are binary and unary operators depending on the number of elements or records an operator acts on. In database searching there are Boolean and Proximity operators. Boolean operators are a subclass of logical operators (Logical operators are binary operators that manipulate data at the bit level.). A Boolean operator manipulates the binary value "true/false".

Periodical index - an alphabetized listing of works that are published at regular intervals of more than one day.

Plagiarism - the passing off as your own, the work of others'. Original sources are not given credit.

Primary source - the originator of a primary record. A primary record is a resource created by the same people that initially experienced or used it. They create the records for their own purposes, records that often remain unpublished. Sometimes they witness an event, sometimes they are involved in an event, and sometimes the record is directly created by the event.

Record - an individual entry in a database and simultaneously a collection of related data fields. Each field, although related, is of a different type to all the other fields in the record (and this is what differentiates a record from an array).

Reference Service - the personal assistance provided to the library users in finding information. All the functions performed by a trained librarian employed in the reference section of a library to meet the information needs of patrons (in person, by telephone, or electronically), including but not limited to answering substantive questions, instructing users in the selection and use of appropriate tools and techniques for finding information, conducting searches on behalf of the patron, directing users to the location of library resources, assisting in the evaluation of information, referring patrons to resources outside the library when appropriate, etc. are regarded as the services provided under library reference services.

Review article - a periodical article that describes, analyses', and criticizes a book, journal article, movie, or other creative or academic work.

Scholarly article - an article, usually in a scholarly journal, that deals with academic subject matter at an advanced level.

Search strategy - a generalized set of technique used in the process of determining what information you currently have, determining what information you need, and determining how to get it. Some possible strategies include; controlled vocabulary searches, specific entry searches, browsing, general scanning, broad to narrow searches, adjacent item browsing, subject tracings searches, keyword searches, citation searches, literature searches, cross reference searches, and chat room questions and other direct people contact searches.

Subject directory - an hierarchical grouping of related subject headings. The tree structure shows relationships between subject headings. They can be found either inside a database or separate from a data base.

Subject heading - the name of the category that a record is included under. For example, the record "natural frequency of vibration" might be found under the subject heading of "Acoustics", and acoustics, in turn, might be found under the subject heading "Physics".

Thesaurus - a book of synonyms, often also containing antonyms. An example is Roget's Thesaurus. In database searching, a thesaurus strategy is to use multiple iterations to search for related words and generate results. The database will often suggest synonyms and related words to try.

Truncation - the shortening of a search word, field, or record. In the case of truncating a search word, this is a strategy used to search among multiple variants or spellings of a word. The asterisk (*) is generally used as a wildcard to replace a letter or letters. An example is invest* which will pick up instances of invest, investor, investments, investigations, etc. In some databases the asterisk must be accompanied with a number that define the number of characters that can be truncated.

Zip - to compress a data file using PKZIP software or some other utility capable of compressing data into PKZIP format. When such a file is restored to an uncompressed format, it is said to have been *unzipped*.

Zoomorphic initial - a figure initial in a medieval manuscript or early printed book composed wholly or in part of forms recognizable as animals or imaginary beasts. Zoomorphic initials are common in the *Book of Kells*. Click here to see a griffin in the the shape of an "S" in a 13th-century German psalter (Getty Museum, MS Ludwig VIII 2) and here to see an example in a 13th-century English Bible (Bodleian Library, MS Lat.bib.e.7). Click here and here and here and here to compare 11th- and 12th-century examples (courtesy of the British Library's *Digital Catalogue of Illuminated Manuscripts*) with this initial D in the 15th-century *Hours of Dionora of Urbino* (British Library, Yates Thompson 7) and this initial A in a 15th-century Italian antiphonal (Metropolitan Museum of Art). Zoomorphic motifs are also used in decorative line fillers, borders, and bas-de-page scenes. Compare with anthropomorphic initial and zoo-anthropomorphic initial.

Bibliography

Albanese, A. (2000b), "The e-book enterprise: netLibrary's digital mission." *Library Journal* 125(3), pp. 126-128 (online). Retrieved March 5, 2001 from *ProQuest* (database). Bell & Howell.

Ali, Nazim (1989), "Science and technology information transfer in developing countries." *Journal of Information Science*. V15, nl.pp. 81-93.

Amold, S.E and Rosen, L.(1989), "Network myths and realities". In *Managing the New Electronic Information Products*. Riverside Data 1989.

Anon (2001b), "Electronic books in libraries: Rights of libraries and publishers." *Information Outlook* 5(2), p. 37- (online). Retrieved March 4, 2001 from *ProQuest* (database). Bell & Howell.

Ardito, S. (2000), "Electronic books: To "e" or not to "e"; that is the question." *Searcher* 8(4), pp. 28-39 (online). Retrieved March 3, 2001.

Armstrong. S J. and Large, J.A.Ed. (1989), CD-ROM Information products: An evaluative Guide and Directory. Information Automation Ltd., Gower, Haris U.K.

Balas, J. I. (2000), "Developing library collections for a wired world." *Computers in Libraries* 20(6), p. 61- (online). Retrieved February 18, 2001 from *InfoTrac Web: Expanded Acadèmic ASAP Int'l Ed*. (database). IAC, Vendor: Gale Group, daily updating.

Barnard, S.B. (1999), "Libraries and e-books: Opportunities and issues." *Future of Print Media Journal* (Spring), (online). Retrieved February 10, 2001 from the World Wide Web http://www.futureprint.kent.edu/articles/barnard01.htm

Breeding, M. (2000), "NetLibrary, innovative interfaces to add e-books to library collections." *Information Today* 17(4), pp. 1-3 (online). Retrieved March 7, 2001 from *ProQuest* (database). Bell & Howell.

Bryant, E. (2000), "E-book summit highlights progress, but slights libraries." *Library Journal* 125(18), pp. 12-13 (online). Retrieved March 5, 2001 from *ProQuest* (database). Bell & Howell.

Burk, R. (2000), "Don't be afraid of e-books." *Library Journal* 125(7), p. 42- (online). Retrieved February 18, 2001 *InfoTrac Web: Expanded Academic ASAP Int'l Ed.* (database). IAC, Vendor: Gale Group, daily updating.

Butcher, Karyles (1990), "The rewards and trials of Networking". Database V13 (4), August 1990. pp.103-105.

Caudra, Association (1991), *Directory of Portable Database*. V3 nl, April 1991. Gale Research Inc., London.

Cibbarelli, Pamela (2003), ILS marketplace: CIL's quarterly series on library automation markets: January 2003: public libraries. *Computers in Libraries* 23 (1): 31-36.

Cline, L. (2000), "Buying electronic: the development of the electronic book market in academic libraries." *Library Collections, Acquisitions, and Technical Services* 24(2), pp. 312-315 (online). Retrieved March 3, 2001 from *ScienceDirect* (database). Elsevier, daily updating.

Coyle, K. (2000), "Change, change, change: libraries and the future." *The Australian Library Journal* 49(1), pp. 27-30.

Crawford, W. (2000), "Nine models, one name: Untangling the e-book muddle." *American Libraries* 31(8), p.56- (online). Retrieved February 12, 2001 from *InfoTrac Web: Expanded Academic ASAP Int'l Ed.* (database). IAC, Vendor: Gale Group, daily updating.

Darnton, R. (1989), What is the history of books? In *Reading in America*. ed. C.N. Davidson. John Hopkins University: Baltimore.

Dillon, D. (2000), *A two year journey with e-books: The University of Texas Experience,* (Web page). The General Libraries: The University of Texas at Austin. Retrieved February 26, 2001 from the World Wide Web: http://www.lib.utexas.edu/cird/principles.html

Ditlea, S. (2000), "The real e-books." *Technology Review* 103(4), p. 70- (online). Retrieved February 18, 2001 from *InfoTrac Web: Expanded Academic ASAP Int'l Ed.* (database). IAC, Vendor: Gale Group, daily updating.

Doering, David (2002), The network observer: it's all about access. *EMedia Magazine* 15 (7):23.

Dorman, D. (1999), "The e-book: pipe dream or potential disaster?" *American Libraries* 30(2), p. 36- (online). Retrieved February 23, 2001 from *InfoTrac Web: Expanded Academic ASAP Int'l Ed.* (database). IAC, Vendor: Gale Group, daily updating.

Duranceau, Ellen Finnie (2001), Tracking content changes at aggregated websites for serials. *Serials Review* 27 (1):51-57.

Engelen, Jan, Evenepoel, Filip and Wesley, Tom (2000), Surmounting the copyright hurdle: the SEDODEL project. (Secure Document Delivery for Blind and Partially Sighted People). Final report April 2000.

European Community (2001), Directive 2001/2G/EC of the European Parliament and of the Council on the harmonisation of certain aspects of copyright and related rights in the information society:

Ferguson, S. (1994), *INF401 Information Society: Module 1.* Charles Sturt University: Wagga Wagga, NSW.

Fialkoff, F. (2000), "Where's the library model?" *Library Journal* 125(13), p. 78- (online). Retrieved March 4, 2001 from *ProQuest* (database). Bell & Howell.

Fiander, M. (2000), "Bringing eMonographs into the digital library: A report of an ALCTS preconference." *Library Collections, Acquisitions, and Technical Services* 24(2), pp. 274-276 (online). (3 Mar. 2001). Retrieved March 3, 2001 from *ScienceDirect* (database). Elsevier, daily updating.

Flowers, J.L. (1999), "netLibrary.com: Cautious optimism / views from a research library and a university press." *Against the Grain* 11(5), p. 22 & p. 24.

Frost, William J. (2002), The Internet Collegiate Reference Collection. *Internet Reference Services Quarterly* 7 (1/2):123-130.

Frumkin, Jeremy (2002), Guest editorial: balancing the playing field. *Information Technology and Libraries* 21 (1):2.

General Libraries, The University of Texas at Austin (2000), E-books update & future plans. *Library News* (August), (online). Retrieved February 26, 2001 from the World Wide Web: http://www.lib.utexas.edu/About/news/librarynews10.html

Gibbs, N. (1999-2000), "E-books: Report on an ongoing experiment." *Against the Grain* 11(6), pp. 23-25.

Greiner, L. (2000), "PDAs are perfect for e-books." *Computing Canada* 26(8), p. 18- (online). Retrieved March 7, 2001 from *ProQuest* (database). Bell & Howell.

Hawkins, D.T. (2000), "Electronic books: a major publishing revolution." *Online* 24(4), pp. 14-28 (online). Retrieved February 17, 2001 from *ProQuest* (database). Bell & Howell.

Ketchell, Debra S. (2000), Too many channels: making sense out of portals and personalisation. *Information Technology and Libraries* 19 (4):175-179.

Kinnell, Margaret, Yu, Liangzhi and Creaser, Claire. (2000), Public library services for visually impaired people. Report to the Library and Information Commission. Loughborough: Library and Information Statistics Unit.

Kirkpatrick, D.D. (2000), The struggles over e-books abound, though readership remains elusive. *New York Times* (Nov 27), (online). Retrieved March 4, 2001 from *ProQuest* (database). Bell & Howell.

Kristl, C. ed. (2000), "Should libraries jump on the e-book bandwagon? (interview)." *American Libraries* 31(7), p. 61- (online). Retrieved February 12, 2001 from *InfoTrac Web: Expanded Academic ASAP Int'l Ed.* (database). IAC, Vendor: Gale Group, daily updating.

Lamont, M. (1999), "Critical human factors in emerging library technology centers." *Library Hi-Tech* 17(4), pp. 390-395.

Landoni, M. & Gibb, F. (2000), "The role of visual rhetoric in the design and production of electronic books: The visual book." *The Electronic Library* 18(3), pp. 190-201 (online).

Landoni, M., Wilson, R. & Gibb, F. (2000), "From the Visual book to the WEB book: The importance of design." *The Electronic Library* 18(6), pp. 407-419 (online).

Loacker, Elsa M. Streamlining the exchange of duplicates. Lib. jour. 66: 381-3, May 1, 1941.

Lonsdale, R.E. & Armstrong, C.J. (2000), "Electronic scholarly monographs: Issues and challenges for the UK." *Learned Publishing* 13(1), 15-24 (online).

Lowell, Mildred H. College and university library consolidations. Eugene, Ore., Oregon state system of higher education, 1942.

Lunin, L.F. and Scimpma, P.B. ed. (1988), "CD-ROM for information storage and retrieval. *Journal of the American Society of Information Science*,V39(1), pp. 31-33.

Maack, I. (2001), "The ebook phenomenon: Is print dead?" *internet.au* (64), pp. 58-63.

Machell, Jean. (1996), Library and information services for visually impaired people: national guidelines. Share the Vision/ Library Association. London: L.A. Publishing.

Mercer, L. (2000), "Measuring the use and value of electronic journals and books." *Issues in Science and Technology Librarianship* (Winter), (online). Retrieved February 26, 2001 from *ScienceDirect* (database). Elsevier, daily updating.

Minkel, W. (1999), "E-books zapping their way to library network." *School Library Journal* 45(11), p. 18 (online).

Minkel, W. (2000), "The e-textbooks are coming." *School Library Journal* 46(9), p. 18- (online).

Morgan, E.L. (1999), "Electronic books and related technologies." *Computers in Libraries* 19(10), pp. 36-39 (online). Retrieved February 17, 2001 from *ProQuest* (database). Bell & Howell.

National Assembly for Wales. (2001), Comprehensive, efficient and modern public libraries for Wales: standards and monitoring.

Pastore, Michael. 30 Benefits of Ebooks, *Epublishers Weekly*, 2008.

Peters, T. (2000), *Charleston Conf. notes re: e-books,* (Newsgroup). Posted as message number 72 by Hoeth, Kathleen on Nov 10th 2000 to news group swfln. Version 21 Apr. 2001.

Quint, B. (2000), "NetLibrary offers 1,500 e-book titles to 100 large public libraries in trial program." *Information Today* 17(3), pp. 18-19 (online).

Rietdyt Ron J. (1988), "Creation and distribution of CD-ROM databases for the library reference desk". *Journal of the American Society for Information Science*. V39(1), January 1988, pp. 58-62.

Ritzier, Claus (1989), "Database on CD-ROM". *IAALD Quarterly Bulletin*, V34(1). p. 5.

Robertson, S., Jitan, S., & Reese, K. (1997), *Web-based collaborative library research.*

Index

■■■